FIND YOUR RIGHT JOB

ANALYZE YOURSELF; LEARN THE PROFITABLE
OCCUPATIONS CONGENIAL TO YOUR CHARACTER.

George S. Clason

CHAPTER ONE

There are certain occupations which each individual is more efficient at than any other. Psychologists tell us that we are all entitled to earn our bread at labor that is pleasing to us, and furthermore that we cannot be contented at any other kind. Economists tell us that the man who is happy at his work produces far more than his discontented neighbor, and does so with less effort and less fatigue.

In brief, the work at which you are most efficient is the kind of work that you like to do and at which you can accomplish the most. It is likewise the work in which you can find the most happiness, make the most money, achieve the greatest measure of success, and do the most good for your fellow man.

Everyone should, therefore, work at a job, occupation, or profession that he likes. Yet, inconsistent as it seems, eighty percent of the people of the world are dissatisfied with their jobs. The reader of these lines may be among the number. The insurance man wants to be a poultry fancier. The public accountant believes he would be better satisfied if he were a traveling salesman. The bookkeeper is certain that if he had only qualified as a plumber he would have been better off - - and perhaps he would! And so on, *ad infinitum.*

Dissatisfaction with one's work is usually due to the fact the malcontent actually is in the wrong line of endeavor. It is possible that the discontented public accountant would actually be better off, financially and otherwise, if he were selling insurance. The insurance man, who may be making a bare living, perhaps would discover his real forte if he were to engage in poultry raising. As for the bookkeeper, it is certain that many men who post ledgers for a living are by nature "cut out" for plumbers; his longing, therefore, may be well-founded.

Thousands of boys are "pitchforked" by well-meaning parents in occupations for which they are utterly unfitted. Some mothers, for instance, are traditionally fond of urging their sons to become ministers, just because in their minds there is something romantic about such a profession. Fathers plan legal careers for their boys because a lawyer is regarded as "somebody" in their communities. The doctor may plan a career in medicine for his son for the reason that "it runs in the family." The uneducated man who "never had a chance" is determined that "my boy's going to have his," and slaves to give his son an education probably far removed from the boy's natural instincts and tendencies.

A square peg will not fit a round hole. Neither will a round peg fit into a square hole. The principal trouble is that most persons, in choosing a vocation, look at the hole only; they fail to take into consideration the size and shape of the peg. Herein lies the trouble, the reason that millions of people in this country are working at trades, vocations, and professions distasteful to them.

There is no necessity for this almost universal discontent. There is no reason why endeavor, or labor, should be monotonous or grinding. Work should not be uncongenial; in fact, the right kind of work should be far more enjoyable than the mere indulgence in so-called pleasure, since pleasure will pall; congenial work, never. The "right man in the right job" is the happiest man in the world. If you don't believe it, pick out any man you know to be happy and ask him why. Nine times out of ten he will name, among other reasons, the fact that he is happy in his work.

UNCONGENIAL WORK WAS RUINING THIS BOY

You may think because you dislike to work, that you are lazy. The writer has in mind the case of a young man whose parents thought this of him: "He hates work," the father declared angrily. "He'll crawl out of it every chance he gets. He's no good."

Inquiry developed that the kind of work the boy "hated" was studying law. Observance of the lad developed the fact that he was, in appearance, the mechanical type. Questioning brought out the revelation that he was "crazy" over machinery. Upon advice of an interested friend, the boy was permitted to drop his legal studies and to take a correspondence course in applied mechanics. All his former indolence was swallowed up in a glowing enthusiasm totally foreign to what his father and mother had believed to be his nature. He eventually qualified as one of the brainier and most resourceful mechanical geniuses in the United States.

Are you a "square peg in a round hole?" Are you discontented with your lot in life? Do you dislike your work? If so, this booklet will help you to discover the vocations in which you can be happy and successful and toward which you should aim. If you are already in your right place, it will tell you that also, and you will be more contented for knowing it.

"Vocational analysis" is a new science that has heretofore been used only by experts. In this booklet it is presented for the first time, available to the average man and woman. The reader of these lines may now determine, for himself, the occupations for which he is best fitted, and at which he can make the most money. There is no guesswork about it. Vocational analysis is not a theory, but a science that has been thoroughly demonstrated. You can prove its efficiency for yourself in your own individual case. You can prove it in the case of your children, your relatives and your friends.

THE GREGORY SYSTEM OF VOCATIONAL ANALYSIS

The system of vocational analysis presented here is simpler than any other method of achieving similar results. It is the result of years of study by Mrs. Ida L Gregory, for twenty years assistant judge of the famous Juvenile Court of Denver, Colorado.

Mrs. Gregory has successfully guided hundreds of unfortunate human misfits into prosperous walks of life. She has analyzed many defective children and skillfully determined lines of work at which they could become self-supporting in spite of mental and physical handicaps. So expert is she in reading human nature that she can tell from a photograph the occupations one should pursue. She has developed a system by which to do this, so simple that any one can learn to use it, and so accurate that it never fails to show the broad, general lines along which lie the opportunities for success for each and every individual.

Mrs. Gregory's system is based upon a knowledge of Character Analysis, a science older and more generally understood than Vocational Analysis. She makes a knowledge of character reading the working principle to determine vocational tendencies. You will be taught in these chapters how to analyze people by their appearance, the first step in determining the kind of work they are suited for.

Character Analysis tells us there are but five basic types of people. Each one of us is either one of these basic types, or, much more probable, a combination of two or more of these. Each basic type has certain tendencies and characteristics almost wholly its own. If we are a combination of more than one type, we have the characteristics of the combined types. Some combinations are complementary, retaining the full strength of the original tendencies; others are not so harmonious and tend to tone down or neutralize these tendencies.

TYPE IS THE FATE THAT RULES US

The five basic types of men and women are determined by heredity. We are so born. We can control and develop our natural traits of character, but we cannot change them. If you belong to a certain type, you will carry the likes, dislikes, preferences and desires of that type with you from the cradle to the grave.

Types vary widely in families; brothers and sisters differ radically from each other and usually fail to know the reason why. One brother may be aggressive commercially, the head of a great business institution with thousands of people under him. Another is a famous preacher, while the third sticks the old, worn-out farm and won't leave the hardship and penury such a life carries with it for any inducement. These men are different types. The man who is an executive probably shuns publicity and works out problems in a secluded office. The preacher craves excitement and approbation, while the farmer finds in the familiar atmosphere of his old home a satisfaction not to be measured by price.

These three men are directed and controlled by the characteristics of their types. The business brother probably could not be hired for love or money to stand in his preacher brother's pulpit and face an audience. The preacher would be a failure in business and neither one of them could any more be coaxed back onto the farm than the farmer could be made efficient in their professions.

To understand your type is to understand your impulses, to realize why you like and dislike, to know why you do certain things so easily and others so poorly, and to grasp the key to your future success.

The purpose of this work is to help you FIND YOUR RIGHT JOB. To do this it is necessary to find out first what kind of a person you are according to your type. In the following chapter you will be explained the five basic types of people and their characteristics.

CHAPTER TWO

THE FIVE BASIC TYPES OF PEOPLE
The Appearance, Action and Tendencies of Each

"A man's a man for a' that", wrote the famous Scotch poet, Robert Burns. Just so, a man's a man and a woman's a woman no matter to which of the five basic types of people they may belong as classified by modern science. However, types makes very different kinds of men and women and science now tell us why they are so different.

In our physical makeup we have five dominant faculties. The first and most primitive of these is the stomach and digestive tract. Some people have more efficient digestive apparatus than others; they care more for their food and handle it better after it has been eaten. This predominant ability to digest has a decided influence on that individual's character forming the first type.

A second type is indicated by a deep full chest giving large lung and breathing capacity, developing characteristics in the individual quite different from the first type.

The third has an unusual development of the muscles, giving exceptional strength and endurance.

The fourth excels in the size and weight of the bony framework or skeleton, usually being taller than other people.

The fifth type of super-development is found in the head and shows in an unusual width above the ears, denoting certain faculties not possessed by the brains of the other types.

The five types will now be described in the above order, showing their faculties, characteristics and distinctions.

THE STOUT OR ALIMENTIVE TYPE

It may be that "no one loves a fat man", but there is no real reason why this should be so, and certainly it does not apply to the fat women. The fat people are the happiest and best married of all. They laugh the loudest and the oftenest. Without them this world would be gray indeed. The stout or alimentive people are so called because of the perfect development of the digestive organs.

The typical fat person in the basic type is a trifle below average height with small bones and soft flesh. The body is large around the waist. The hands and feet are puffy. The face is round with childish features. The complexion medium or dark.

The stout type loves comfort, comfortable clothes, cozy chairs and plenty to eat. They are acquisitive because they want creature comforts. Therefore, they long for luxuriant homes. They are self-indulgent and, when able, gratify every longing. They are not fond of exertion and would be indolent, were it not necessary to work for the good things they crave. When smart, they get others to do the hard work for them.

They enjoy humorous reading, plays other amusements, and are generally fond of the lighter music.

In the trades, the stout type is usually engaged in the handling of foods as cooks, butchers, grocers, etc. In the combination types we find them in high places in finance, business and the arts. They combine to excellent advantage with all the other types. People of this type are more often just plump and well rounded than grossly corpulent.

THE ANIMATED OR THORACIC TYPE

The animated type with their large lung capacity and strong heart action are the most emotional and excitable of the five basic types. In appearance they are the most handsome as well. From this type and its combinations come the great majority of the theatrical and movie stars. In many current magazines can be found typical pictures of this type of people with their clear-cut, attractive features.

Usually having blonde complexions, they are by nature quick and active, of medium height, with trunks and arms longer than normal and short legs. The hair is usually light, light brown, golden or red; the cheeks red; and the eyes grey, blue or green.
They flush and blush readily. The fingers of the hands are artistic, tapering at the ends. As a type, they are restless lovers of pleasure and excitement. They must have social life and are unhappy in isolation. They are sensitive, high-strung and frequently temperamental. They require change and must be engaged in occupations that give an outlet to this natural desire. They are clever and adaptable, learning quickly and throwing up an uncongenial job with a speed that is the despair of the employer who places them at work to which they are not suited.

This is a valuable type, as from it we get the true artistic strain and the basis of higher salesmanship. Industrially they cling to the arts or artistic merchandise. They are the best dressers of the five types. At the time the Greeks built their marble temples, they were a blond race.

THE MUSCULAR TYPE

Here we find the workers of the world. The MUSCULARS with their compact body square-set and below medium height, are the men and women who most efficiently man our shops and factories, dig our trenches and do those Herculean tasks required to take care of modern civilization, tasks that call for physical strength and the skill to handle tools of every description.

The MUSCULAR face is oval, the sides straight and parallel, the neck thick and strong. He has a broad chest and shoulders. His hands are particularly characteristic, being square with broad, short fingers. His complexion is dark or medium.

The MUSCULARS are quick workers, forceful and determined, often pugnacious. In the basic type they almost invariably work for others. In combinations they become executives, army officers, writers and inventors. Muscular women make capable and efficient wives and can be identified by oval faces. As a rule the MUSCULAR is content and dependable; but when he takes a notion to travel, he moves unhesitatingly for long distances. His kind was well represented among the trail-breaking pioneers.

THE BONY OR OSSEOUS TYPE

The BONY people can usually be recognized at a glance because they are normally tall and thin. Everyone above normal height has the bony characteristics, and these are as outstanding as their physical appearances. BONY people are noted for their conscientiousness, persistency and honesty. They have been the martyrs who died for religious convictions. They were the type of the Pilgrim Fathers who were content to settle the bleak New England coasts. They are frugal and self-denying, small eaters, caring little for personal appearance or social customs. They can live happily in isolation, and in this respect are just the opposite of the animated type.

Small BONY people can be identified by the prominence of their cheekbones and the length and thinness of the neck.

The BONY people are slow to think and move, but very careful and accurate in what they do. They share with the MENTAL type the honor of solving the world's mathematical problems. They are well-poised and self-contained, firm in their own convictions, and not easily influenced. The basic type are natural farmers, stock raisers and prospectors. Combined with the mental, they have given us some of the greatest men of history, such as Ford, Rockefeller, Lincoln and many others. The complexion of the BONY type is dark or medium.

THE MENTAL OR CEREBRAL TYPE

The MENTAL type can be recognized at a glance because they are undersized with frail bodies and large heads. Above the ears, the head bulges widely, sloping to a narrow chin.

Temperamentally, the MENTALS are timid and retiring, caring little for what they eat or how they dress, and avoiding, if possible, crowds and social life. They are natural book lovers, storing their minds with knowledge which they too often have no way to use.

When employed at work at which they can use their brains, they are *good* workers, having great endurance and unusual powers of concentration. At physical labor they are weak and inefficient.

The MENTAL does not possess any more intelligence and common sense, if as much, as the other types. He has a mentality, however, of a different character. He can analyze, plan and originate in a way entirely foreign to the normal minds of the other types. He is a valuable addition to their faculties. In combination with other types, the MENTAL characteristics show to their best advantage. In the basic form, the MENTAL is the most helpless and most unhappy of all. If uneducated, he lacks a practical way to make a living, being unable to compete as skilled labor, and is often found in most humiliating occupations.

Mental types, more than all the others, must be suitably educated to achieve happiness and success.

CHAPTER III

HOW THE TYPES COMBINE

Characteristics of the Combinations

For the convenience of the reader, in this work we will hereafter refer to these basic types not by their anatomical names, which are often confusing, but by their typical characteristics, thus: STOUT, ANIMATED, BONY, MUSCULAR, MENTAL.

The reader who wishes to make a correct vocational analysis must be able to accurately classify the person by type or combination. The pure types easily recognized, as are many of the simple combinations. But the more combinations that exist in one individual, the more difficult the task of proper classification and the better all around personality.

Careful study is urged of this chapter. If in doubt do not trust to appearance alone, but by questioning find out whether type tendencies exist that do not show distinctly in appearance.

Also bear in mind that no two people are exactly alike. If we classify them correctly according to their type or combination, we must also take into consideration the relative proportion of each type in their particular make-up. Thus, two men may be STOUT-ANIMATED, one dominantly fat, the other dominantly animated. The first would be more strongly influenced by the STOUT characteristics, which would be moderated somewhat by the ANIMATED. The second would be influenced the stronger by the ANIMATED characteristics and approximate closely that basic type. Therefore, a person may not care for certain occupations for which the analysis shows him to be fitted. Salesmen and ministers are often closely allied in type, but far from interchangeable in ambitions and desires. After type is determined, natural preference must not be ignored in determining vocations.

In combination types we find the strongest, most aggressive characters. Theodore Roosevelt, for example, was MUSCULAR-ANIMATED-STOUT-MENTAL, possessing, therefore, physical strength, nervous energy, and a reflective, analytical mind

Type, however, cannot determine the amount of mentality any more than it can determine physical strength. Another man who is MUSCULAR-ANIMATED-STOUT-MENTAL may do well to hold a position as a waiter or barber, because he lacks mentality or education, although being the same type as Roosevelt. Type can determine the kind of work that each individual will enjoy and for which he is best fitted. It cannot and should not be expected to guarantee the measure of success that the individual can achieve, for this is a question to be determined by individual mentality, strength of desire to succeed, and the amount of education of a right kind to bring out the type strength.

CHARACTERISTICS OF THE COMBINATION TYPES

When one person is a combination of several types, that person naturally has the characteristics of each type represented. Some characteristics blend like the artistic sense of the ANIMATED, simply being an addition to the other type characteristics. Other characteristics, like the economical streak of the BONY, do not harmonize with the self indulgence of the ANIMATED; and where these types are combined we find usually a person less free to spend than the ANIMATED, yet more liberal than the BONY, a modification of the instincts of each.

Here is a brief list of the dominant characteristics of each type, reduced to the fewest possible words, with a suggestion of what each type usually adds in a combination.

STOUT: Good-natured, easy-going; Fond of comfort, self indulgence, acquisitive. In combination, it adds good nature and the desire to own properly to enjoy the good things of life and establish financial independence.

18

ANIMATED: Active, changeable, artistic, social, aesthetic, self-indulgent, free spending. In combination, it signifies more "pep", love of the artistic, and sociability, with greater tendency to be changeable and unstable.

MUSCULAR: Quick, orderly, diligent, mechanical, skilful, strong, provident. In combination, it increases skill with the hands, strength, orderliness and diligence, aggressiveness, combativeness.

BONY: Slow, conscientious, self-denying, persistent, frugal, opinionated, unsocial. In combination this type impregnates seriousness of thought and purpose, accuracy, conscientiousness and economy.

MENTAL: Timid, sensitive, retiring, unsocial, studious, analytical, frail, persevering. In combination it adds knowledge, analysis, imagination, originality, resourcefulness, and refinement.

CHAPTER IV

THE THIRTY-ONE KINDS OF PEOPLE

What They Look Like - - How to Classify Yourself

The following list gives the usual appearance of the five basic types and the twenty-six possible combinations in which these types may occur.

Each type and combination is given a number. When you determine your true type or combination, check the number, for in the following chapter of Profitable Occupations these numbers are used to refer to the different types suitable for each occupation. After properly classifying yourself and finding your number, you can thus tell exactly those occupations in which you are best fitted to succeed.

1. STOUT: Slightly below medium height. Fat, soft flesh; small-boned. Range in fleshiness from mere plumpness to heaviness. Round-faced with childish features. Fat hands and feet. Large waist. Dark or medium complexion. In appearance and action, Walter Hiers, screen comedian, is typical of this type.

2. ANIMATED: Usually light-complexioned. Light, golden or reddish hair; blue, grey or green eyes. Occasionally brunettes. Blush easily. Often red on back of neck. Long body and arms, with short legs. Medium height and weight. Tapering fingers. In appearance and action, Eva Tanguay, actress, is typical of this type.

3. MUSCULAR: Below medium height; square shoulders, solid body. Thick neck; round, solid arms and legs. Rectangular face, straight on sides with rounded chin and forehead. Square hands. Dark complexion. Douglas Fairbanks is typical of the MUSCULAR.

4. BONY: Above medium height; generally tall and raw-boned. Large feet and hands with long fingers. Rectangular face with pronounced cheek and jawbones. Long neck. Dark complexion. Lewis Stone, screen star, is typical of this type. SMALL BONY the same except for height.

5. MENTAL: Small, frail body; small neck. Large, wedge-shaped head, wide above the ears. Small, narrow chin, delicate hands. Sallow or dark complexion. Lloyd George and Judge Ben B. Lindsey both prominent thinkers, of this type.

6. STOUT-ANIMATED: About medium height. Stout, but flesh more firm than in STOUT type and bones heavier. Face longer and hands not so puffy, with fingers longer. Fairly active. Complexion light and skin ruddy. Madame Schumann-Heinke, singer, is typical in appearance of this type.

7. STOUT-MUSCULAR: Below medium height. Stouter than the MUSCULAR, but not so soft as the STOUT. Round face, square shoulders; strong and active. Dark complexion. John McCormack, popular tenor, typifies the appearance of this type.

8. STOUT-BONY: Above medium height. Usually a big fat man with dark complexion. Varies from rotundity to big-waisted, flabby fat. Broad, firm face. Slow and deliberate in action. President Harding was typical of this type.

9. STOUT-MENTAL: Typical in appearance to the STOUT type, but more refined. Below medium height. Intelligent face with head broad above ears. Clear cut features. Dark complexion. Herbert Hoover is of this type.

10. ANIMATED-MUSCULAR: An athletic type with blond complexion and trim, muscular body. Medium height. Quick, nervous and active. Type, Caruso, the famous tenor, and the popular Mary Pickford.

11. ANIMATED BONY: Above average height, usually tall, slender blondes. A common type that can be recognized on sight. SMALL ANIMATED-BONY: slender, with prominent cheek and jawbones. Lionel Barrymore, actor - tall, slender, fair - is a good example. Also Sarah Bernhardt.

12. ANIMATED-MENTAL: Medium height or below. Body rather slender, with delicate hands and small feet. Light complexion. Delicate face. Head wide above the ears. Walker Whitesides, actor, a good example.

13. BONY-MUSCULAR: Above medium height. Rectangular face. Stocky-built people. Dark complexioned. Jack Dempsey is typical in appearance.

14. BONY-MENTAL: Above medium height, usually tall, raw-boned, with head bulging above the ears, often with large features. Dark or medium complexion. Abraham Lincoln, Henry Ford, John D. Rockefeller and Susan B. Anthony are well-known examples. Judge Landis is of the SMALL, BONY-MENTAL type.

15. MUSCULAR-MENTAL: Stockily built, below medium height, with bulging head. More delicately built than the MUSCULAR, with slender hands and smaller neck. Dark or medium complexion. General Grant, Premier Clemenceau, and John D. Rockefeller, Jr., can be taken as typical.

16. STOUT-ANIMATED-BONY: Above medium height. Substantial blondes. Usually rather of firm flesh, without excessive fat. Refined faces. Well-shaped hands and feet, fingers long. Hobart Bosworth, screen actor, typifies this combination.

17. STOUT-ANIMATED-MUSCULAR: Medium height or below. Light complexions. Moderately fat, but nervous, strong and active. Broad, substantial bodies with square shoulders. Fritzi Scheff, vaudeville star and comedian, is a good example.

18. STOUT-ANIMATED-MENTAL: Below medium height. Light complexion. Slightly fat, but graceful and active. Refined faces, good features. Head high and broad. William Alan White, author, belongs to this type, also Carrie Chapman Catt, suffrage leader.

19. STOUT-BONY-MUSCULAR: Big, substantial people, only slightly fat with firm flesh and well-muscled arms and legs. Hands large and broad. Dark complexion. The famous John L. Sullivan was exactly this type.

20. STOUT-BONY-MENTAL: Above medium height with mental heads. Usually fat, slow and inactive physically, but active mentally. Dark complexion. President Cleveland typified this combination.

21. STOUT-MUSCULAR-MENTAL: Below medium height. Fat and rectangular in appearance. Flesh firm. Muscular face with mental head. Refined features. Dark complexion. Ex-Senator Simon Guggenheim is typical of this combination.

22. ANIMATED-BONY-MUSCULAR: Above medium height with solid, rectangular bodies. Strong and unusually active for large persons. Light complexions. James J. Corbett is a well-known example.

23. ANIMATED-BONY-MENTAL: Above medium height, usually tall, genteel-appearing blondes. Slender, graceful and active physically. Refined face; mental head. Slender hands with tapering fingers. General Pershing, George Washington, and President Wilson were all of this type. Cardinal Gibbons also, although small.

24. ANIMATED-MUSCULAR-MENTAL: Below medium height. A well-built, genteel light-complexioned person. Graceful and active. Typical MUSCULAR body, but lighter in weight. Mental head. Refined features, small hands and feet. Samuel Gompers and Billy Sunday are both good examples.

25. BONY-MUSCULAR-MENTAL: Above medium height with the bulging, mental head. Refined features. Active and skillful. Dark complexion. Thomas A. Edison is our best-known example.

26. STOUT-ANIMATED-BONY-MUSCULAR: Heavy people, above medium height. Rectangular build with firm flesh. Light complexion. Unusually active for large people. Example, Charles Murphy, famous leader of Tammany Hall.

27. STOUT-BONY-MUSCULAR-MENTAL: Square-built people, above medium height, with solid, fat flesh. Dark complexion. Big, square hands. Bulging, mental head. President Taft is representative of this combination.

28. STOUT-ANIMATED-MUSCULAR-MENTAL: Medium height. Light complexion. Active, well-poised, alert. Muscular development usually more pronounced than the stout. Mental head. President Roosevelt and Chief Justice White were good examples of this balanced type.

29. STOUT-ANIMATED-BONY-MENTAL: Above medium height, with mental head. Active mentally, but slow physically. Flesh soft. Fingers slender. Face refined. Charles Schwab is a well-known man of this four-type combination.

30. ANIMATED-BONY-MUSCULAR-MENTAL: Above medium height with mental head. Unusually active for large people. Refined and genteel in appearance. John Barrymore, actor, is typical of this combination.

31. STOUT-ANIMATED-BONY-MUSCULAR-MENTAL: Here is the all-around person combining the five types and being the rarest of all combinations. Average height or slightly above. Light or medium complexion. Plump, rectangular body. Mental head. Refined features. Genteel in appearance. David Starr Jordan, educator, and William Jennings Bryan, are both examples, although quite different in personal appearance.

HOW TO FIND YOUR RIGHT NUMBER

To determine your right number in the preceding list, make a chart for yourself similar to the one below. Write upon it your personal appearance, putting under each heading those physical features that correspond to the types as described in Chapter II. Do the same with your other characteristics. It is your strong type traits that determine your best abilities. Minor traits are merely influences. So mark off those physical and mental attributes not strongly pronounced. Get down to your basic classification as closely as possible. See what types you have strongly marked and find the key number for the combination of these.

STOUT ,Appearance ....
Characteristics ....

ANIMATED, Appearance ....
Characteristics ....

MUSCULAR, Appearance ....
Characteristics ....

BONY, Appearance ....
Characteristics ....

MENTAL, Appearance ....
Characteristics ....

CHAPTER V

EIGHTY PROFITABLE OCCUPATIOSN ANALYZED AND DESCRIBED

With Key Showing Suitable Types for Each

The following key gives eighty principal businesses, professions and vocations that offer a good field of endeavor for ambitious men and women. There are many lesser professions, vocations and special businesses which for lack of space cannot be listed here individually, for which the reader can make his own classification by comparison with some similar occupation which is listed. The same type of people will succeed in the same type of businesses.

Type characteristics are the same in men and women, except as they are modified by sex. In business life the sexes are more or less interchangeable. Women of one type will succeed at occupations of the same kind as men of similar types, except as they are barred by physical strength and feminine personalities.

The numbers following the descriptions of businesses listed here refer to the types and combinations of types listed in the preceding chapter. Great discrimination has been used in selecting the types adaptable to each, to include only those best suited to succeed at each occupation. It is not claimed that others also cannot succeed, for this would not be so. For example, take ACTING. Some of the most famous actors and actresses have been MENTAL-BONY, a type not recommended here for that profession. Many people succeed out of their natural lines because of an unusual mentality that should have brought greater success and greater happiness in more suitable occupations. There can be misfits in high places just the same as in lowly.

The four and five-type combinations are known as balanced types or all around people. They can succeed at almost any kind of occupation but if strong characters are not satisfied until they advance to important positions. For this reason they are listed as suitable types only in those occupations offering broad opportunities.

ABSTRACTING

Considered one of the lucrative positions, for persons who will begin at the bottom and work studiously and patiently. Service consists of compiling abstracts of title for the protection of purchasers and mortgagees, to land and other real property; also in looking up patents, deeds and wills, foreclosures of mortgages, judgments in partition, decrees in probate proceedings, and tax sales, liens and other encumbrances. In the United States the abstractor usually confines his investigation to public records, although comparisons of original documents are also essential and helpful. Knowledge of law and commercial law not strictly essential, although helpful. Elementary education sufficient for start, provided individual is of average intelligence. Salaries run from $2,000 to $50,000 a year, for trained men or women, but most abstractors in time become members of abstracting firms and share in profits, bringing average earnings much higher. Great difficulty is reported by abstracting firms in obtaining student abstractors who will stick to work long enough to become proficient. Take a patient and close application. The best method of getting start is to get position in abstracting office, or real estate office with title guaranty department. Accuracy is highly important as a qualification for successful effort. **Suitable types 5-14-15-25.**

ACCOUNTING

One of the growing professions that is not overcrowded, for reason chiefly that a high degree of exact knowledge is essential to success. The expert accountant should be versed not only in bookkeeping, but in the theory and practice of finance, commercial law, and the scientific principles of organization and business management. Degree of "Certified Public Accountant" is conferred by some states, after examination. The service consists in the supervision of books and records of large undertakings, or the occasional verification, analysis and audit of accounts and records, and of devising and installation of new systems of accounts and methods of procedure. Proficiency in this profession requires a mathematical mind, patience and clarity of analysis. May be studied at universities and business colleges. Expert accountants are usually employed on the fee basis. Earnings run as high $50,000 a year, salaries usually from $2,500 up to $20,000 a year, annually. This profession is gained chiefly by practical experience, after mastering elementary features, and continual study while practicing. **Suitable types 5-14-15-25.**

ACTING

Acting can be divided into two general classes: "Speaking", and "Silent." The profession one of most overcrowded in the world, but highly lucrative for those who attain the heights. Stars in vaudeville always in demand; musical comedy stars find steady employment the year around in vaudeville or musical comedy; legitimate actors and actresses usually can depend upon not more than forty weeks employment out of fifty-two, although some obtain special summer engagements at resorts. Burlesque comedy confined mostly to states east of Mississippi. Profession hazardous for great majority in it. Amusement business considered more so than any other, from financial standpoint.

In prosperous times most professional people are employed at fair to high salaries; in times of financial stringency and

28

industrial depression actual hardship is experienced by many. The aspirant to stage honors must be willing to go through long period of discouraging, unremunerative apprenticeship; to encounter rebuffs; to work harder than at most things for less compensation; to sacrifice many of the things that make life worthwhile to the average person, for the sake of possible future rewards. A good education is essential to success in legitimate stage activity, where interpretation of different characterizations is required; not so essential in vaudeville field. Excellent health a prime necessity; proficiency in dancing, fencing, and the simpler forms of acrobatics, including careful attention to physical culture, helpful. Voice should be strong and clear; applicant should have good chest development. Charm and magnetism of personality essential. Handsome appearance essential for some kinds of stage-work; non-essential for others. Proficiency in music, both vocal and instrumental, is a distinct aid to success. In the motion picture field the chief requirements are personal magnetism and charm, ability of pantomimic interpretation, personal pulchritude, vivacity of expression (also mobility), and a face that "screens" well.

There are numerous dramatic, dancing, pantomime and motion picture schools over the country, chiefly in New York and Los Angeles, that claim to train students in the histrionic arts. Some of them are good; many are bad. Dramatic authorities agree that the best method is to gain proficiency by actual experience. Stock companies gathered over the land offer opportunities in many instances. The Little Theatre movement is helping also.

Earnings range from $25 to $5000 per week, depending on the ability and prominence of the individual, but these earnings apply to only a part of the year for the majority. New York is the Mecca for most aspirants, because the managers have their headquarters there. Possession of wardrobes gives the applicant a more favorable hearing from the managers; such wardrobes are strictly essential to employment outside the chorus class. **Suitable types: 2-10-12-24.**

29

The highest type and best-paid dramatic people before the public today are the concert artists. They draw from $100 to $5000 per night and represent the cream of the profession, singers, piano players, violinists, etc. These people have come up through the school of hard work plus natural talent and are in positions worth working for. The singers usually gain their reputation first in grand opera. **Suitable types: 6-10-11-18-21-23-24.**

ADVERTISING AGENCY

Advertising agency requires person well grounded in principals and practices of advertising, with access to specific information regarding rates, circulation, standing, etc., of newspapers, magazines, and periodicals of all kinds, all over the country. An agency cannot be listed as such without official recognition by lending magazines, such as the Saturday Evening Post; to obtain such recognition the applicant must be able to show a certain balance in the bank (usually $5,000) as proof that he will he able to submit with a advertising copy check cover space charge. Agencies usually operate upon a commission basis of fifteen per cent, as compensation, of the space charge, usually paid by the publication receiving the order. Advertising agents should be able to write, or have written, copy for advertisements, and to supply the illustrations for same if required; but principally to know the market so well as to be able to give expert and authoritative counsel as to the character of circulation best suited to the thing being advertised, and to recommend, or to place copy with, publications reaching the market sought at the most economical outlay of expense. The profits of a successful agency may be very high indeed, running as high as $100,000 annually. **Suitable types: 14-15-20-21-23-24-25-27-28-29-30-31.**

ADVERTISING WRITING

Advertising is growing rapidly all over the English speaking world as a business creator in all lines, including manufacturing, wholesale and retail selling, money-raising projects and appeals for man and woman power. A profession almost limitless as to moneymaking possibilities. Thousands of publications of all kinds, in the United States, live by advertising support. Advertising writing requires technical knowledge of typography, printers' terms, etc. The writer should have good judgment as to balance, proper sizes and kinds of headline and "body" type, and psychological appeal. A wide command of English essential, together with ability to exercise proper selectivity and eliminate superfluous words and phrases. Colleges and schools are turning out so-called advertising writers in great profusion; but the writer with the "punch" is always in great demand. Knowledge of subject necessary to good advertising writing: also of merchandise, or whatever is offered for sale. High school education almost imperative; college education
helpful. **Suitable types: 5-14-15-20-21-23-24-25-30.**

AGRICULTURE

The farm offers unparalleled opportunities for the man who is "cut out" for farm life; who loves the soil, is able and willing to work hard and long, who has excellent health, and who takes the trouble to fortify himself with a combination agricultural and business education.

The farm is the basis of national prosperity. Food, clothing and shelter are the three essentials of life: and food is perhaps the most important of the three. The lure of the city is drawing many thousands of young men away from the farms nowadays. They usually make a poor choice, exchanging the fresh air and independence of the country for the hectic hustle and bustle of urban life, with its restrictions, its narrow vistas, its unhealthy adulterations, its tinsel, its glitter, and its too often genteel poverty.

Recognizing the need of expert training and scientific soil knowledge for success in farming, states have established numerous agricultural colleges which annually graduate young men and women fortified with specific knowledge of what might be termed the "chemistry" of farming; who have been taught something of economies, business principles and commercial mathematics; who have learned soil culture and values, and who are able to rotate crop advantageously. The ability to read and analyze the food market is as highly essential to successful farming as the ability to follow a team of horses after a plow or cultivator, according to modern ideas.

The profit in agricultural pursuits is more attractive than many suppose. Periodically there goes up a cry that the farmer is starving; but the fact is that the intelligent, trained farmer, properly financed and equipped, usually is financially successful. **Suitable types: 4-10-11-13-22.**

ARCHITECTURE

Requires men and women with artistic sense, ability to make extensive research, memory for details, judgment and mental balance, patience, vision and executive ability. Young men and women peculiarly eligible, since proficiency in architecture means years of study, application and practice. The graduate from high school should enter an architect's office as an apprentice. Two years in such an office should give him enough practical knowledge and experience to fit him for entrance to one of the schools of architecture, most of which are located in the Eastern states, for a four years' course. College graduates may dispense with the two years' apprenticeship and take the architectural course directly after graduation, two years usually being sufficient to turn out the full-fledged architect.

The most successful architects of the country are those in specialized branches, such as residence, office building, naval, military, ecclesiastical, etc. The more advanced architects become authorities upon different schools, such as the Moorish, Byzantine, Romanesque, Saxon, Norman, Gothic, etc. There are not more than fifty "aristocrats" among architects of America; these men make huge sums of money in what are known as competitive, architectural activities, including great public buildings, cathedrals and memorials.

The earnings of a good architect may mount up to figure. The usual method is to compensate the master architect upon a commission basis, six percent of the total costs of a structure in most states. Out of this six percent, however, the architect may have to pay for engineering estimates and plans, such as the steam heating and plumbing layouts, etc.

The master architect may receive a very large sum indeed for one job; the new state capital at Lincoln, Nebraska, for instance, is said to have paid the supervising architect something like $200,000. **Suitable types: 11-22-23-30.**

ARTIST

The artists in watercolors and oils, also those that specialize in crayons, charcoal, pencil sketches, etc., are liable to have a "hard row to hoe" before they attain eminence in the profession. Long periods of rigid self-denial, hard work and expense must be endured. However, an artist usually takes little heed of these things. If he has the urge within him he will struggle continually to progress, at whatever cost. Only a few artists attain financial heights; even some of the best live from hand to mouth, and often sell their pictures for pitifully small sums. The artist should, if possible, have an independent income and be free from financial worry. Membership in an art class, of which there is at least one in nearly every city or town of fair size, is the best way to start. After that progress depends upon the circumstances and talent the pupil; the costs may run into many thousands of dollars, with only occasional sales to offset this expense. As a career this branch of endeavor cannot be recommended; however, the dyed-in-the-wool artist keeps at it despite the frequent discouragements, and a few of them become well paid. **Suitable types: 10-11-23-24.**

ASTRONOMY

It is not generally known that the field of astronomical research is distinctly a paying one, in a financial way; but such is the case. Competent astronomers are far from plentiful, and colleges and universities all over America are glad to obtain the services of men and women capable of teaching this fascinating science, especially if they are also capable of making observations and calculations based upon them.

Professors of astronomy are paid salaries as high as those paid in any branch of higher education. In addition, astronomers who constantly observe the heavens and planetary systems are in demand as contributors to scientific magazines. These publications pay from five to fifty cents a word for authoritative contributions upon this subject. One contributor has been known to receive as high as eight hundred dollars for a series of such articles, written in a little more than two days.

A college degree is highly essential to the attainment of eminence in the profession. The average astronomer of merit and profundity of astronomical knowledge may command an income of from $5,000 to $25,000 a year. **Suitable types: 5-14.**

AUCTIONEERING

The professional auctioneer thrives principally in the more thickly settled farming districts of the United States and Canada, although in all cities may be found regular auctioneering establishments.

The auctioneer should possess a good voice, excellent lungs, the ability to talk rapidly and distinctly, to gauge human character instantly, and be an expert in sales and crowd psychology. He should be professionally jovial, good natured and energetic. A physical weakling would last but a short time in this strenuous profession; two hours on the auctioneer's platform is exceedingly exhausting, as any experienced auctioneer will testify.

A wide knowledge of all kinds of merchandise, household furniture and effects, kitchen utensils, etc., is required for success in this field. Auctioneers in the cities should be specialists; in big urban centers like New York and Chicago there are auctioneers who know diamonds and fine jewelry as well as professional diamond brokers and jewelers. The same is true of auctioneers who specialize in selling imported rugs, tapestries, etc. Others are experts in the sale of paintings and fine statuary. Auctioneers are paid on a commission basis, which may be as high as ten percent of the total received at a sale.

Live stock auctioneers occupy a field by themselves. Draft horses and the finer specimens of horseflesh are often sold to the highest bidder. Great stockyards always maintain their auction centers, where animals are paraded up and down before buyers, while the auctioneer shouts out their alleged good points. A livestock auctioneer should be an expert upon stock of all kinds, able to judge accurately and instantly the probable value, and to detect blemishes or peculiarities that may hold down the price. Many veterinaries are auctioneers. **Suitable types: 6-16.**

AUTOMOBILE AGENCY

The automobile agency as a business has grown to enormous proportions. In the larger cities palatial salesrooms and immense service departments are maintained for every make of car. Many car agencies are located in the medium sized towns and hardly the smallest village is without one of some sort. The agency for a car calls naturally for a supply and service department and offers fine opportunities for money making to men of good business ability. This is especially true in the larger towns. Such agencies must include in their executive force three distinct types of men: salesmen, superintendent of service, and general executive. Partnerships between men of these types make effective and successful firms. The following types are suitable: Service Department, **13-15-22-24**; Sales, **2-10-11**; Executive, **9-14-15-16-23-24-20-21-25-27-28-29-30-31.**

AVIATION

One of the newer occupations that will take a more important place in the future is aviation. Men who can skillfully guide an airplane are paid liberally. Only comparatively few kinds of people are suitable for this work: **2-10-11-22.**

BAKERIES

The baking business has grown to-large proportions in this country of late years, principally because housewives are neglecting the art of the home baking, and have grown to depend upon the bake shop and the grocer for their daily supplies.

Successful bakers are specialists, save in the cases of those who run small establishments, independently or in connection with retail groceries. One bakery may be expert on baking bread, another on cakes, another on pies, etc. The bakery turns out one of the most perishable of products, and fast deliveries are imperative.

Big baking establishments now have extensive advertising departments; an intelligent and energetic baker may enter the latter and eventually rise to be in full charge of the selling activities, where the compensation compares favorably with that commanded by good salesmen the country over. The proprietor of a big baking establishment is in effect a manufacturer, and must exercise the same care, close attention to business and market knowledge as any other manufacturer. Great fortunes are being made by men of this class. **Suitable types: 1-6-7-18-19-26-28-29**

BANKING

Banking being a particular form of business endeavor, the person contemplating taking it up as a life work must prepare carefully. The banker should first of all be a good mathematician, by instinct as well as by training. He should have a "good head for figures." He should learn commercial law and finance. He may receive his theoretical education and training in almost any college; even high schools now teach the more elementary forms of finance and banking. Business colleges specialize in them. Universities give special courses in everything that pertains to banking. The average banker gets his practical training in a bank, usually beginning at the very bottom. The first position obtained by him may be that of bank messenger. Promotions in most banks come traditionally way of the death of somebody higher up. However, if a young man has made many influential friends through his connection with an established bank, he may be selected to head a new institution being organized; or even to take charge of the organizing activities. This gives him a "short-cut" to a higher place in the banking world, and an earlier chance to make good than he might otherwise get.

The compensation for persons employed in banks is not attractive until the official positions are attained. Tellers, cashiers, vice-presidents, secretaries, treasurers and presidents may receive as high as $10,000 to $100,000 annually, depending upon the position and the size and importance of the institution. A bookkeeper may get from $100 to $150 a month; a junior teller from $125 to $225; clerks from $100 to $125. As in other things, there are exceptions both ways to these salaries, but they are exceptions; not the rule. Banking offers to those of the right types opportunity to rise high, to others only clerical positions of minor importance. **Suitable types for banking executives: 9-14-20-23-27-28-29-30-31.**

BEAUTY PARLOR

One of the newer professions, into which women and girls, and even men, are graduating in ever increasing numbers. At this particular time they are thriving largely because of comparatively recent and radical changes in feminine hair dressing. The popular "bob," of which there are many kinds, bids fair to increase for some time to come. Cosmetics, skin "foods", powders, cold creams and other facial beautifiers are being sold in greater quantities than ever before.

Artists in this line are not numerous, in proportion to the number engaged in it. There are many so-called correspondence school graduates in the business. Genuine knowledge concerning the causes of falling hair, dandruff, dry skin, etc., is comparatively rare. Ability to gauge a haircut and curl by the contour of the face underneath is not frequently met with.

That there is an oversupply of persons in the business of only mediocre skill in the business is evident; nevertheless, the opportunity is there for the one who properly prepares for the profession. The best existing method of starting is to serve an apprenticeship in a shop, gaining in experience daily, meantime reading in spare time authoritative works on care of the hair, scalp and skin as the public library, book store and special college courses may supply.

Compensation ranges from $10 per week, for apprentices (some shops pay nothing at the start), up to $75 a week for experts. Profits depend upon the business ability of the person engaged in it, and upon location and demand, much as they do in other business lines. Apprenticeship usually runs from six weeks to three months. **Suitable types: 10-12-15-17-18-24-26.**

BOARDING HOUSES

In cities, towns, mining camps, lumber camps, etc., there are usually opportunities for the establishment of paying boarding houses, catering to the patronage of single people. Boarding houses are of course divided into classes: the highest class cater to high class patronage, comprising office employees, heads of departments, mercantile establishments, bankers, etc. The lower and medium classes cater to workmen and women who are employed in factories, mines, at common labor, etc.

A successful boarding house keeper should have considerable business ability and be familiar with foods, especially from selection and buying experience. Economy of operation is highly important if any money is to be made. It is a widely quoted saying that most boarding house profits go into the garbage; elimination of waste will usually mean entries "on the right side of the ledger." This means also extreme care in selection and buying, especially of meats.

The field for this kind of business is broad. The aspirant should look about carefully, and select a location adjacent to the places where the prospective customers are employed. If there is not already an oversupply of established boarding houses in the vicinity, the venture may be made with comparative safety. An ordinary establishment may be launched for about $1,000, where all equipment is purchased outright. Many persons rent both house and equipment.

The life means long hours, and does not usually pay large profits for small establishments. It offers a means of livelihood for ambitious women who know how to cook and are capable of working hard, and a steppingstone to the management of profitable family hotels. **Suitable types: 3-7-8-16-17-19-22-26.**

BROKER

The broker may deal in stocks, bonds or commodities, such as wheat, cotton, sugar, coffee, etc. The most reliable stockbrokers deal only in "listed" stocks of recognized standing. Some deal in bonds only, and those secured by first mortgages upon well-established Properties. A broker may buy anything for which he the money or credit, and sell at a profit if his judgment has been good as to the market rising. Or he may handle accounts on "margin," and by selling on a market that is falling make money for his clients. He collects a commission either way, whether the client makes or loses money on the speculation: but the broker who advises a speculation that turns out disastrous is liable to lose prestige, and, eventually, patronage. Hence it is important that extreme care be used in advancing information and advice.

The broker usually begins by personal operations in speculation, thus gaining the experience essential. If he is conservative and moves only after careful deliberation, he has a chance to make money. After getting ahead a few thousands, he may rent and furnish an office and establish himself as a broker, subject to the laws of his state governing such operations. In most states the broker must be adequately financed and financially responsible to his clients, so that his checks will he good when given to clients in payment of stock sold or profits realized on margins.

The field may be compared to that of gambling, in many respects. If the aspirant possesses the requisite daring and courage, and financial conditions generally are good, he may be justified in making the venture in any population center where money circulates freely. Brokers make big fortunes, and if successful at all usually make profits of from $150 a week up to almost any figure. They should be thoroughly grounded in the theory of finances to in success. **Suitable types: 4-11-14-23-30.**

CAMERAMEN

This is the term applied to the photographer who takes motion pictures, usually for the big producing companies of New York and Los Angeles. An expert cameraman is always in demand; in fact, it is virtually impossible to get one upon short notice, since they are under ironclad contracts with large enough salaries to make the signing of such contracts attractive. The way to become a cameraman is first of all to learn photography. The cameraman must know the chemistry of photography thoroughly before he can possibly hold a position with an established motion picture company. In addition, he is required to become proficient in the peculiar art of motion photography, which is ordinarily photography *plus*. When "on a set" the cameraman has no time for experiment.

He must know his business, and know it with such thoroughness that he will waste not a moment in taking a scene, and taking it right. He must be peculiarly adept in gauging atmospheric conditions and the shades of light. The cameraman usually begins as the "camera kid," as the apprentices are called. As he acquires the special brand of knowledge and experience required far successful motion photography, he may qualify as a full-fledged cameraman and command the salary that goes with it. Salaries range from $125 up to $500 a week, far the good ones. The lesser ones may receive from $60 up to $100 weekly. **Suitable types: 10-11-23-24-30.**

CANDY MAKING

The candy manufacturing business is one of the biggest in the country, Americans being admittedly the most prolific consumers of candy in the world. The mystery is, to the layman, that so much of this brand of confectionery can be disposed of before it spoils; for candy is highly perishable, and requires constant refrigeration, natural or artificial, to keep it in sales condition.

It is not necessary for the aspirant to this field of endeavor to start in a large way. Many small confectionery stores exist in all cities and towns, for which the candy may be made in a back room or in the basement. Thousands of men and women who have learned to make candy in big factories open these small establishments, and make a comfortable living from the start. From these small beginnings they may enlarge, until they have factories of their own; for every candy store which makes its own output is in reality a factory, with its distribution system connected directly with the manufacturing end.

Knowledge of materials and how to buy them most economically, combined with experience and skill in manufacturing, plus hard work, should give the candy manufacturer a fair field. The candy business depends largely upon seasonal demand, but can be so conducted as to stay a profit all the year. A few hundred dollars will start one in a modest way. **Suitable types: 1-6-7-8-16-17-19-26.**

CARTOONIST

There is no royal road to success in this calling, unless the aspirant has the cartooning "bug", however he will probably sooner or later attain more or less success; but the outstanding cartoonists of the country with big incomes, can be counted on the fingers of the hand. Below them are hundreds of lesser aspirants, all striving to climb higher. No longer do the leading newspapers employ cartoonists to draw the big "picture" which appears in the center of the first page, daily. A few have clung to the practice, but the majority now use their funny artists to illustrate humorous "stories" written by staff reporters. Such artists as "Bud" Fisher, creator of "Mutt and Jeff," Sidney Smith, of "The Gumps," and George McManus, of "Bringing up Father," make immense incomes; that of Fisher is said to approximate $500,000 a year.

The best method by which the aspirant may get a start at the profession is to join an art class, of which there usually is at least one in every city of fair size. Now and then a professional cartoonist may be found who will accept a few personal pupils, at moderate fees. Occasionally one "breaks in" merely by practicing in secret and submitting, by mail, samples of his work; this method is not recommended, however, as it is seldom successful. Ordinary cartoonists and funny artists may make from $25 to $250 a week, depending upon experience and the size of the paper. Cartoonists employed by the humorous weeklies and monthlies in the United States and Great Britain, as well as in Canada and Australia, get from $100 a week up. Incongruous as it may seem, the laugh provoking pictures are produced by a serious type of men, students of the psychology of humor. **Suitable types: 11-14-23**.

CHIROPRACTIC

There is but one effective method of acquiring proficiency in the science of chiropractic and that is via the chiropractic college. Chiropractic is a comparatively new science, which teaches the healing of disease and ailments by a system of adjustments of spinal vertebra and manipulation of different parts of the anatomy. It is a drugless system of therapeutics, claiming to heal virtually every known disease, especially those not actually organic. Thousands of young men and women are entering the profession annually, graduating from the schools of chiropractic over the country. About fifteen percent are held to be really competent with enough scientific knowledge of anatomy to entitle them to be classification as "skilled." Highly skilled chiropractors in many cities earn as high as $60,000 annually; others make a bare livelihood. The code of ethics in this Profession is different from that of *materia medica* in some respects, especially as regards advertising. Chiropractors generally have no scruples against professional publicity and advertising; those who advertise the most widely and effectively usually are those who make the most money. The profession is not overcrowded as yet, especially with really skilled adjustors, but it is rapidly becoming so. Its sponsors and supporters claim that as a science it is still in its infancy. More and more people are becoming converted to it as a remedial and preventative agent. About three to four years are required as a study course; personal attendance at the school being essential. **Suitable types: 3-7-10-12-22**

CONTRACTING

Buildings, roads, railroads, street paving, sewers, etc., are largely built by contractors, who often sublet different portions of the work to subcontractors. So many different things enter into the construction of even a small dwelling that one supervising head is highly essential. The building trades include carpenters, stone masons, brick layers, plasterers, lathers, stair builders, floor builders, inside finishers, plumbers, steam fitters, electricians, wiring experts, painters, etc. Each of these is a separate trade, and if the man building the house at his own expense were to attempt to handle them all, he would encounter grave difficulties in the majority of cases. Hence, the contractor is an important man, who by long experience must be familiar with all the trades, and with the class of men representing them. He must, first of all, be able to handle men. He should be able, also, to calculate and plan. He may have plans to guide him, but he must be able to gauge and judge these plans intelligently, and to read specifications with a wise and understanding eye. He must know materials. It is highly essential that he be familiar with costs of materials, since he takes his contract usually at a flat price, and stands to make or lose in proportion to his judgment and alertness in buying his materials and labor.

The contractor need not be a highly educated man, although a practical education is great aid. He should possess a mathematical brain and a practical head. A contractor is a distinct type. He must be able to gauge and judge mankind and mankind power, and to be a "driver" without actually driving his men to the point of sulking. He obtains his contracts usually by entering his bids in competition with others, these bids being accompanied with plans and specifications. The contractor must state, in his bid, the price at which he will undertake to do the work, which price usually includes the materials and labor costs. He must also be prepared, especially in large undertakings, to give a bond as surety that he is financially able to go through with the contract. Thus it will be seen that a contractor must have considerable financial responsibility; as well as courage and daring.

The business can be highly profitable and the field wide and varied. It offers innumerable opportunities not only in construction work but in doing any job that can be estimated, purchasing material, etc. **Suitable types: 11-16-18-22-23-25-26-27-28-29-30-31**

CONSUL AND DIPLOMAT

The diplomat needs to have diplomacy in the every day affairs of life, if he is to succeed in the field of professional diplomacy. The man without this qualification should look elsewhere for a career, since one diplomatic blunder may involve the country represented in serious difficulties.

The diplomat must be well educated, and if possible cultured. Nothing less than a college education will suffice. It is true that consuls and vice consuls sometimes lack such education; but they are seldom successful in the fullest sense of the word. Many men Professionally or commercially successful in private life enter the diplomatic field, not so much for the money as for the honor and experience, and perhaps for the pleasure of travel to foreign countries.

Young men with stenographic or secretarial experience are often chosen by the appointed consul, charge d'affaires or ambassador to accompany him upon his diplomatic mission. As a career, therefore, the diplomatic field is divided into two classes. The consul or ambassador may be a man who has previously had no experience or training whatever as a diplomat; but he will surround himself with an experienced staff if he is wise. Hence, by far the larger class is that entered by young men and women ambitious for a career in diplomatic service, rather than in diplomatic representation.

They will be chosen to go with the chief to the country to which the latter has been appointed; frequently such employees remain in the post for long periods, serving several chiefs.

As a career, diplomatic service does not offer large remuneration, the pay ranging from $125 a month up to about $275. Acquaintance with a man newly appointed as consul or ambassador may be valuable, since it may result in an offer of employment. After one has gained some experience in the work, he or she is quite certain of more or less steady employment thereafter, since diplomatic service is specialized, and persons without the experience are seldom qualified to take part in it. Political "pull" or influence is usually essential to employment, as it is to appointment to a diplomatic post. **Suitable types: 5-1-9-18-28.**

DAIRYING

This is distinctly a career for a specialist. Success is for the person thoroughly experienced in the care of cows, scientific feeding and the maintenance of sanitary environment for such animals. In America cleanliness and health are enforced in most dairies, virtually all cities having ordinances designed to regulate the industry and protect the babies from the menace of impure milk. In some places the competition in the dairy business is not keen; in others the field is vastly overcrowded. Adequately equipped dairies, fairly well capitalized, usually make good money. Business methods help immensely to bring profitable results. The dairy business renders a distinct service to the community, one which it would he impossible to dispense with. The aspirant should by all means first learn the business by working for some established dairy, for wages. **Suitable types: 4-8-13-19-26.**

DANCING

Of late years there has sprung up all over the United States what may be termed a "craze" for specialty dancing, especially of the classic and Interpretative school. Thousands of children are being trained in dancing schools and classes, upon the theory that such training builds good health and makes the pupil graceful. This "craze" may at present be merely a fad, which may die out in a few years. Or it may develop into a permanent expression of American social life, and thus afford a profitable field for the teacher of such dancing. In any event, such schools are increasing rapidly, indicating that at present there is money to he made in the field.

Dancing may be divided into two branches: Teaching and professional performing. In New York, Chicago and some other population centers, schools for the teaching of professional dancing have existed for years. Pupils who graduate from these schools sooner or later obtain engagements, after which their advancement in dancing as a career is strictly "up to them." In addition to learning the intricate and complex steps and movements, the dancing pupil must exercise the most rigid self-restraint as to diet, take strenuous aerobatic exercise and must be prepared to work very hard to attain proficiency. There is no easy road to this proficiency; the dancer cannot "get by" on bluff. Theatrical managers are keen businessmen, who make their money in a hazardous profession, and they employ talent strictly upon merit. It takes from two to five years to turn out a proficient, professional dancer. After gradation the dancer must train and practice daily, to keep the muscles adequately flexible.

Professional dancers may earn from $75 weekly and up, depending upon ability. Some stars command princely salaries, ranging as high as $2500 a week.

The teachers of dancing are like other business persons, making money in accordance with the extent of their business ability, the character of community in which they are situated, etc. Suffice it to say that this appears to be an excellent field for profit at this writing, and probably will continue so for some time to come. Of course, no one can conduct a dancing school unless he is himself master or mistress of the art. **Suitable types: 3-10-13-22.**

DENTISTRY

This is one of the most profitable professions and is annually growing more so, despite the fact that every city has from dozens to hundreds of dentists. It is still in the formative stage, although dentistry is known to have been practiced as long ago as 500 years B.C. It has emerged from the crudities which characterized the practice a hundred years ago, into a professional science second to none, and dentists are rapidly gaining for themselves recognition as contributors to the will being of society in no uncertain way.

The profession has grown to such proportions, in fact, that many dentists specialize in distinct branches. There are, for instance, the "prosthetic", or mechanical dentists, who specialize in laboratory dentistry, making plates for false teeth, bridges, etc. Others specialize in filling, bridge and crown work; others in extracting, and still others in the administrating of anesthesia.

The student of dentistry must become proficient in the knowledge of the structure, physiology, and pathology, as well as the therapeutic, surgical, and mechanical treatment of the tissues of the mouth, and its contained organs; also of the materials used, and their manipulation in the restoration of the dental and oral structures. In the earlier part of the dental courses as given by numerous dental colleges in the United States, the student is required to study anatomy, bone structure etc., much the same as the student of medicine and surgery. In fact, the modern dentist is apt to become an expert surgeon, so far as operations in the mouth are concerned.

Roughly, about four years must be taken to fit one for practice. A successful practicing dentist may clear from $300 to $1000 a month, or even more. **Suitable types: 10-11-22 23-24-30.**

DETECTIVE WORK

The most successful detectives of criminals are those who graduate from the ranks of the police forces, later becoming identified with established detective agencies as "operatives". It is a wide field, and a profession that cannot be learned by study of correspondence courses, advertisements of correspondence schools to the contrary notwithstanding.

There are agencies which specialize in "shadowing". Rich men frequently employ such agencies to shadow their wives, whom they suspect of misbehavior. Rich wives do likewise. Men and women seeking for evidence upon which divorces may be obtained may use the detective agency for this purpose. Many agencies specialize in tracing lost and wandering persons, for a consideration.

The detective should be a quiet individual, careful and guarded in his utterances. He should be constantly observant, and have the faculty of remembering peculiar facial blemishes and characteristics. Peculiarities of walk and carriage must be watched and noted. A detective should have what is termed a "camera eye"; that is, he should be able to retain in consciousness a picture of the person under consideration; he should, in fact, be able to pass such pictures before his mind's eye at will, as a panorama.

A detective should be courageous, also, since there may be times when he must face real danger. No timid man should ever engage in this profession, which at time is hazardous. The best detectives have at least high school education; not a few are college bred. The better the education and training, the better the detective's chances to rise to the top of the profession, where the monetary rewards are sometimes very high indeed.

One branch of detective work is found in the government postal inspection department. The pay in this department averages about $3,000 annually, the chiefs drawing proportionately more. Several years service in the post office department in other lines of activities are required, the inspectors being drawn from the ranks. Postal inspectors may be sent to all parts of the country in pursuit of their duties; they are even sent to foreign countries on occasion. The government secret service is still another branch employing high class, well paid men.

A police detective is paid whatever the civic service rules of his particular city may provide; usually it runs about $200 to $250 a month. Operatives in private agencies get about $50 to $60 dollars weekly, with expenses for traveling and hotels when on the road. Chiefs in agencies get as high as $350 a month; railroad special agents from $175 to $300 monthly. Managers of agencies may get enormous fees, running as high as $20,000, for a single case; but the latter may take months for completion, and the manager must pay the expenses of maintaining his agency and employing operatives, out of the fee. A successful detective who has made a reputation may command almost his own fee, since he is sure to have more work offered him than he can possibly handle. **Suitable types: 2- 4-5-11-12-23.**

DOG FANCYING

A successful dog fancier must be an authority on pedigrees, blooded dogs of all kinds, and must keep pace with the demands of the hour as to dog popularity. Years ago, for instance, the "pug" dog was most in demand, despite the fact that it was undoubtedly the ugliest of all canines. Just now, the Boston Bull Terrier, the Pomeranian, the German Police dog, and the Airedale divide the honors about equally. What the style will be five years from now one knows; but whatever it is, the successful fancier must know it, and be prepared to fill the demand satisfactorily.

A dog fancier should both understand dog nature and love dogs. He should be thoroughly familiar with dog anatomy. He should know how to breed and feed scientifically, in addition to which he should be a keen businessman and salesman.

The most successful dog fanciers have small farms, where they build and maintain their kennels and "runs". A dog must have plenty of fresh air, exercise and the right kind of food. A dog kennel is necessarily a noisy place, especially at times; therefore the fancier should locate it as far from places of human abode as possible, and still he able to serve his market.

Fancy prices are paid for fine hunting dogs, also dogs of the protecting variety, as well as the more ornamental breeds. There is no oversupply of dog raising talent in the field, since the fancier must he born with a love and instinct for dogs, in addition to putting in a long apprenticeship in the training and care of the animals. Any one desiring to engage in dog fancying as a career should first obtain employment in some established kennel, where he will become familiar with dog habits and professional methods of caring for dogs. Dog fanciers seldom make great fortunes, but hey enjoy their work thoroughly. **Suitable types: 4-11-13-16-22-26.**

DRESSMAKING

Good dressmakers are traditionally scarce. The profession is one of those cited in economic philosophy as profitable because they are so unpopular. All women desire to have their clothing made to their individual order; few care to do the work.

Dressmakers usually have all they can do, in the cities. In fact, they are liable to have more than they can accomplish satisfactorily. They must be expert seamstresses, cutters and fitters; frequently they must be designers as well, and must possess the faculty of selecting patterns and designs best suited to the peculiar type of women under consideration.

The great stores of the larger cities, and many of the smaller ones, now have regular dress making departments, used chiefly for alteration purposes. The head dressmaker in such a department may receive as high as $150 a week, or as low as $50. Seamstresses, cutters, fitters, etc., receive from $18 to $35. Designers are in demand, and may earn from $50 to $200 weekly, depending upon the size and importance of the establishment.

Men predominate as designers and fitters, women as seamstresses, both fancy and plain. Bath sexes are represented in the cutting branch of the profession. There are now many colleges over the country teaching dress making in all its branches: but the apprentice system is still the most in vogue, the apprentice entering an established shop and working for little or no compensation, in order to learn the business. A bright pupil may learn enough of dress making in six weeks to obtain a position, at fair wages, in a dress making shop. The tuition ranges from $60 to $300. As in other fields of endeavor, greater proficiency is attained with longer study and practice. **Suitable types: 10-11-22-23-24-30.**

DYEING AND CLEANING

This is essentially a business of service. The man or woman starting out in it cannot hope to succeed unless fortified with experience in the trade; otherwise the service given may be faulty, and trade will fall off even before it gets a good start.

There are no great fortunes to be made in this branch of endeavor, save in rare instances, but it can be built up into as successful a business as the average service business, however, prospering in proportion to the energy, initiative, integrity and good judgment that is put into it. A good pressing machine, table and dyeing and cleaning equipment will cost approximately $2,500. The dyer and cleaner should have at least one delivery wagon or truck, to start, as a part of the service system. A capital of at least $3,000 is essential. **Suitable types: 14-15-20-21-25-30.**

ELECTRICITY

This is a subject so vast in magnitude, and so diversified in its application, that it would be impossible in the space allotted here to more than sketch it. Electricity is the greatest motive force in the world today, and the greatest transmission force. Science frankly doesn't know what electricity is; it is simply a mysterious force in the air about us, which appears to he illimitable in supply, scope and power.

The man who takes up the study of electricity will be able to take his choice of a large and increasing number of specialties, from operating a trolley car to operating the wireless apparatus on an ocean liner. Radio, the latest phase of electricity, presents an excellent field for the aspirant.

All correspondence schools, technical and trade schools, and many colleges and universities now offer courses in applied electricity. The aspirant can only be advised here to follow his instincts in selection of the branch he desires. It is a highly fascinating branch of endeavor, with its possibilities only scratched at this stage of the world's development.

Great power and transmission corporations, of which every city in America has at least one, employ many thousands of men as electricians. Virtually every urban home is now equipped with electric lights, doorbells, etc. Electric heating apparatus is increasing in general use. Many big hotels now cook with electricity exclusively. Automobiles must he equipped with electric batteries, for starting the motors, lighting the lamps, operating the signals, etc. Thousands and hundreds of thousands of miles of telegraph and telephone wires form a network over the continent. Steam trains are lighted with electricity. The country has great systems of electric railways, both urban and interurban. Messages are transmitted from one country to another via wireless and ocean cables.

In the field of therapeutics electricity is being utilized increasingly. The up-to-date physician will have electrical apparatus as part of his equipment. Electricity is being employed in treatment of the scalp and hair.

Men of brains, industry and intelligent application may find in this field excellent opportunities for congenial occupation and remunerative employment. It is obvious that thorough preparation is necessary, since no position can he held by "pull." The field is not overcrowded, since new discoveries and successful experiments are taking place almost daily, causing the scope of this branch of activity to widen constantly. **Only a limited number of types seem to succeed in this field: 11-22-23-30.**

ENGINEERING

This branch of activity includes civil, military, mining, mechanical, electrical and experimental engineering, which in the early days of the practice all came under one head - that of "civil" engineering, as distinguished from "military." Briefly, engineering is the practice of specializing in the analytical study and building of buildings, bridges, water works, tunnel projects, irrigation systems, roads and railways, light houses, retaining walls, shore apartments, buildings, etc. The mechanical engineer specializes in the designing and building of machinery and engines of all kinds. The electrical engineer may specialize in designing and building telephonic, telegraphic, power generator, transmission electric railway and lighting equipment, and in electro-chemistry. There is also the branch of engineering known as "experimental", in which the practitioner does research and laboratory experimental work, for the purpose of solving problems which come up from time to time in engineering practice.

As a profession, engineering is highly interesting and absorbing. Engineering colleges and universities all over the country have turned out so many graduates of late years that the field may be said to be overcrowded. The government employs many hundreds of them, at only fair salaries. The engineer usually is one who loves the peculiar character of his work, however if he does not, he would better remain in some other occupation. The engineer must be thoroughly educated and trained in his profession; his college course alone taking four years, and his postgraduate work perhaps years longer.

Engineers who have reached the top of the profession may make as high as $50,000 a year. For one of these, however, there will be hundreds who are fortunate if they are paid $2,500 and $3,000. The cost of preparation is seldom less than $3,000, including tuition, and very close application to studies is imperative. **Suitable types: 11-20-14-23-30.**

EXECUTIVES

Executive ability is in demand and big business is willing to pay well for it. Executive ability means the ability to handle people, to organize affairs and through the combination of both to accomplish results. It should not be confused with the desire "to boss," common to many people who possess neither vision nor congeniality. A man may be a successful businessman, yet a poor executive. In that case he succeeds best by employing executives. Men and women possessing this rare gift should by all means associate themselves with a large business where they have an opportunity to learn and develop. **Suitable types: 9-15-20-21-26-27-28-29-30-31**

FLORIST

The successful florist loves his work and everything pertaining to it, unless it be the strictly business part. However, once a greenhouse is established, the business end may almost take care of itself. Seldom is any advertising on an extensive scale, soliciting or any of the usual methods of "drumming up" necessary. If the florist thoroughly understands his work, and the science of plant culture, he will produce the flowers and plants that the people want.

The florist should study botany, of course. He should work around flowers all his life, if he would be successful. An apprenticeship in a greenhouse is valuable for the man expecting to own a greenhouse of his own some day. The culture of all the popular flowers, in season, is essential. The Easter, Christmas and Mother's Day seasons are especially productive of profitable business for the florist these days. Cut flowers were never before in so general a demand. Funerals, weddings, church festivals and social affairs help to make the demand for flowers of all kinds more or less constant the year around.

The field is good and the financial returns large enough to make the venture worthwhile for the man or woman who love this peculiar kind of work. There is considerable competition, but not so much as in many other lines, owing to the extensive and accurate knowledge required. **Suitable types for flower store: 10-11-12-15-23.**

FURRIER

With the growth of surplus wealth in the United States, and the corresponding increase in the wages and salaries paid toilers in all lines of endeavor, the fur business has taken on new importance of late years. Where in former times only the very wealthy could afford to wear genuine furs, now women and girls much lower in the financial and social scale are able to indulge in this luxury. The field has been greatly widened by the "summer fur" style. Furriers are springing up all over the country.

The successful retailer in fur garments should be able to remodel, and should be an expert judge of fur values. The aspirant should aim to learn all about the different kinds of furs, their wearing qualities, stylishness, etc. Relatively few employees of furrier establishments possess complete information regarding their stock in trade. Superficial knowledge is altogether too much the rule. The aspirant who takes pains to learn all about furs stands a chance for rapid and profitable advancement.

Fur remodelers may earn as high as $60 a week; but expert and clever fur salesmen, who are usually paid in commission in addition to salaries, may earn up to $100 a week in season. The best are selected to travel for the wholesale fur houses, at salaries averaging $300 monthly, besides commissions. Many are paid from $3,000 to $7,500 a year.

The aspirant who secures employment with a retail furrier may in time decide to enter one of the wholesale houses or factories, as a further activity in the acquiring of a fur education. The field is good and the chances for profit equally so. **Suitable types: 4-10-14-20-25.**

GARAGE

This is a highly important branch of the automobile industry, and growing more so daily. The autoist caught far away from home with a sprung axle, a blown-out tire or serious engine trouble, knows that the thousands of garages scattered over the country are literally "lifesavers". Garage owners need not necessarily be mechanics, but knowledge of mechanics is a distinct aid. Many garages now have exclusive district agencies for the sale of widely known makes of cars, and build up profitable business two ways thereby.

Location is important. In cities, garages are scattered all over town, including the suburbs and residential districts. In small towns they are usually close to the center of the business district, on the road of which the main street will form a part. Garage men depend largely upon transient patronage for their business, although they may also build up a solid, regular patronage, based on painstaking and competent work and service. Sales of gasoline and oil may go far to swell the total receipts; storage charges, which run from eight to twenty dollars a month in the majority of cities, are generally expected to pay the rent or part of the "overhead". **Suitable types: 7-21-23-26.**

GEOLOGIST

As a student of the structure of the earth's crust, the modern geologist is in great demand far his knowledge concerning oil, mineral and other deposits. No group of capitalists would think of investing in mining or drilling ventures without first having a geological survey made of the field under consideration, save in cases where a "strike" has already been made.

The geologist may command a good income, in the form of fees. His ability to determine the composition of rocks, association of minerals, disposition of straits, etc., has a cash value. The invention and wide manufacture and sale of the automobile has brought geologists in keen demand by capital seeking to develop oil fields. Many famous strikes have been made following drilling operations based upon geologists' reports.

The government Geological Survey employs large numbers of expert geologists, at good salaries. Experience gained in the numerous surveys sponsored by this department enables many geologists to earn large incomes after leaving the federal service.

The geologist may fix his compensation on a fee basis, the fee depending upon his reputation for accuracy in making geological reports and predictions based upon his findings. Or he may be employed by a syndicate or corporation of capitalists on a straight salary, which will run from $5000 to $10,000 a year. Some geologists make as high as $25,000 annually, especially in times of mineral or oil excitement.

Courses in geology are given by all state universities and many lesser schools and colleges. About four years' study are required before the geologist may regard himself as qualified to enter the practice. **Suitable types: 14-23-24-30.**

HOTEL MANAGEMENT

This is a profession by itself, and is annually drawing more and more men and women into its ranks. An experienced hotel manager will always find his services in demand, at a good salary. The best hotel managers usually graduate from the commissary department. They need not have any practical experience in cooking and preparing food; but they should be expert buyers, which means that in the formative stages they should serve as hotel stewards. The hotel steward must do the actual buying, but he is supervised in this duty by the manager, if the latter knows his business, save in cases where the steward is so reliable as to require to watching.

Hotel managers have reputations for getting profitable results are continually being offered better posts, at substantial increases in compensation. Close attention to the details of the business, long hours, the ability to bear responsibility, quick thinking in emergencies, and buying experience are the requisites for success, coupled with a faculty for handling "help". The hotel manager, in other words, must be a businessman in every sense of the word.

Compensation is usually based upon the earnings of the hotel, with the manager receiving a guaranteed salary and commission on gross receipts over a prescribed minimum. The average manager should make about $250 to $500 a month, with his board and room included. Managers of the metropolitan hotels in large cities receive up to $25,000 a year.

Employment as a steward or assistant, in a moderately large hotel, is to start in this business, since successful hotel managership is impossible without thoroughly practical experience. **Suitable types: 6-9-17-18-28.**

ILLUSTRATING

Here is a calling holds forth many alluring aspects for the aspirants, provided they possess the requisite talent and willingness to put in a long apprenticeship. Commercial artists are in great demand, and the demand is growing with almost incredible rapidity. All large department stores, of which there are now many hundreds in the United States and Canada, have their commercial departments in connection with their advertising departments; medium to large daily newspapers maintain similar departments as well, while large establishments especially in the industrial cities employ large numbers. A good commercial illustrator may take his pick, literally -- always bearing in mind that he must be good. There is no place in the commercial art world for an indifferently trained artist. Through preparation is requisite to success.

The commercial artist must learn to draw accurate reproductions of many kinds of merchandise, such as shoes, men's suits and overcoats, women's wear, dresses, etc. The human figures used in commercial advertising need to be idealized and usually elongated. Wash drawings and line work are employed principally, although some establishments go much further. Swift action and sure strokes are essential; the commercial artist must be able to fill a "hurry up" order promptly.

As with cartooning, membership in an art class is a good way to get a start in this profession. A pupil with promising talent may be given a junior position in the art department of a store or newspaper at little or no salary.

Salaries of commercial artists run up to $100 a week on daily newspapers, and about the same figure in the advertising department of advertising and mercantile establishments. Magazine illustrators, or artists connected with the big advertising agencies that specialize in placing advertising with the nationally circulated magazines, may draw as high as $500 a week; some of the stars get more. **Suitable types: 12-23-24-30.**

IMPORTING

Hundreds of millions of dollars worth of goods and commodities are imported into the United States annually from foreign countries, and sold here at a profit. They include such things as coffee from Brazil, sugar from Cuba, cotton from Egypt, Sheffield steel articles from England, jewelry and diamonds from Holland and Paris, toys from Germany, clothing from England and France, olive oil from Italy and Greece, tea from China and

Ceylon, silk from China and Japan and other items too numerous to record here.

In order that these importations may be disposed of profitably and expeditiously, it is necessary that they be handled in this country by people familiar with the market at both ends of the line, the languages, foreign exchange, etc. Such persons are called "importers". They do business on a commission, or buying and selling basis, and usually make plenty of money in times of peace and international prosperity.

The importer must have connections at the other end of the line with an exporter who may be a member of his own firm, or be in business for himself. Payment for goods purchased for importing purposes are made with bills of exchange, redeemable in the money of the country from which the purpose is made. This means that the importer must know exchange values at all times, and learn the intricate workings of the foreign exchange system.

The importer usually does business on a wholesale basis, selling his purchases to the "trade". He is therefore in relatively the same position as the manufacturer and wholesaler of domestic goods, in that he must be in constant touch with the demands of his market and be able to gauge correctly the probable demand for any imported article he contemplates ordering. Upon his knowledge of the market, and upon his accuracy of judgment, depend the profitable character of the transaction. The importer should have all the qualifications of a large businessman, and in addition have large experience in this particular branch of activity. Without such experience he would be lost.

Many importers get their start from being employed in offices or warehouses of importing concerns, and thus acquire the requisite knowledge and experience to enable them to open up a business for themselves. The importer has the chance to build up a big business with a large annual profit. Employees in importing houses often attain good positions at good salaries, if they become proficient and especially if they learn foreign languages.

Such persons are frequently sent to foreign countries to buy for the home firm. **Suitable types: 9-10-14-15-20-2221-25-27-28-29.**

INSURANCE

There was a time when the "insurance agent" was regarded as a necessary evil, a pest that everybody dodged if possible. He was in the same category as the undertaker. But that time is now past; today the insurance man is one of high types of businessmen, who make big incomes and live in luxury. It is probably the highest form of salesmanship, with the possible exception of real estate.

The aspirant to a position in the insurance world should have at least a high school education; a college education would be better. The successful insurance salesman should approach big and wealthy men and women, as prospective customers for what he has to sell, and he should therefore have the confidence which through academic training ought to give. Perhaps in no other line of endeavor does a knowledge of psychology play so important a part. The insurance man has no samples, in the commonly accepted meaning of that word. He must be a character analyst, if he would achieve the greatest measure of success, and be able to study the prospect shrewdly and scientifically.

It is not difficult to get a start at this profession. Almost any agency, of which there are thousands in America, will give an applicant a chance, especially if he measures up to integrity and appearance requirements. All agencies maintain schools in which the rudiments of insurance salesmanship are taught. Many women are making a success as insurance saleswomen. Agents arc usually started out on commission, with a small drawing account to pay immediate expenses; later, and as they advance to higher positions, they are given good salaries and commissions. Supervising agents may draw commissions on all policies sold with their territory, regardless of who makes the actual sale.

Salaries and commissions may range from $15 a week for beginners; to $1,000 a week for experienced experts. **Suitable types for salesmen and executives: 11-14-20-23-25-27-29-30-31.**

JOBBING

A large part of the merchandise sold by the retail merchant is purchased from the wholesaler or jobber. The wholesaler acts as the middleman between the manufacturer or producer and the retail dealer. Extensive business experience is required to successfully enter the jobbing business in the established lines of drugs, groceries, paints, hardware or dry goods, as well as ample capital. It is, however, a profitable and genteel field well worth the attention of ambitious men. May be entered by branching out in a modest way from a retail business and building up a jobbing business on the side or through employment or purchase of an interest in an established institution. **Suitable types: 9-14-15-20-21-23-24-28-29.**

LAWYER

Because law is one of the oldest and most dignified of the professions, it attracts more thousands of aspirants annually than can possibly be sustained by it. However, the fact that even poor lawyers make a living, and often a very fair one, should be sufficient incentive for the aspiring young man, or even young woman, to look upon it with favorable eyes. The aspirant should be very sure of at least two things before he launches forth upon the legal career. One is that he really desires to study and practice law. The other is that he is vocationally fitted for such a profession. A course of four years, for sure, is necessary to insure the student a diploma and entrance to the bar. Among other qualifications, the lawyer should be well educated, have marked forensic ability (although many lawyers specialize as "office attorneys", seldom appearing in open court), a good voice, and what is known as legally analytical mind. A mind for details and the ability to sense their significance are essential. The lawyer should have finely attuned perceptive qualities; he should have the faculty of concentration to a marked degree. He should be thoroughly grounded in the principles of law, both federal and state.

Most lawyers specialize in criminal, civil or commercial law. These are distinct branches, although co-related in many respects. "Jury" lawyers are proficient in eloquent and persuasive appeals to juries, as the title implies. Some lawyers excel in arguing motions; others in the examination and cross-examination of witnesses. Still others are know as the "diggers"; that is, they possess an exceptional talent and faculty for untangling knotty points and problems of law, by virtue of recourse to decisions of other courts and tribunals, which they site as "authorities", and to the session laws of state.

As the independent lawyer works strictly on a fee basis, his income depends upon his ability, acquaintance and reputation for legal success. The usual way is to demand a "retainer"; that is, a certain sum of money paid over in cash, which has the effect of effectively pledging the lawyers to the side of the person employing him, regardless of larger offers which he might receive from the other side. The retainer is a guarantee of the responsibility and good faith of the litigant. Civil lawyers may demand a fixed fee, or may, in the case of suits for money damages, accept a percentage of the damages obtained. The latter method is known as the "contingent fee" plan. Most lawyers, even in small communities, make not less than $3,000 annually to $5,000. The stars of the profession may make as high as $50,000 in a single case. **Suitable types: 5-14-15-23-24-25-30.**

LAUNDRY

This is a "service" business, in which attention to details, pride of achievement, adequacy of machinery and of delivery system are the most important things to be considered. There is no dearth of laundries; nevertheless, there are many in the field which do not deliver first class service, and still appear to be financially successful. Therefore it may be assumed that there is room for the aspirant who has business ability and expert knowledge.

Primarily, the laundry business is simply one of washing and finishing linen and other washable fabrics, and doing it well and quickly. But to do these things requires a smoothly working establishment, modern machinery, experienced help and a capital investment of at least $10,000. $20,000 is really nearer the average. Up-to-date methods of soliciting patronage are also required. The laundry that gains a reputation for good work - - that is, clean work with the least wear and tear on fabrics and which does not lose work entrusted to it, has a good chance for success, other things being equal.

Although there are cases on record where financial success has been attained by persons who entered the laundry business without previous experience, the latter is usually very important indeed. Such cases are rare. The man with organizing ability may start by surrounding himself with other men of the requisite experience, and by applying fundamental principles of business succeed from the start. Such a man should be able to command or organize capital, however. Some comfortable fortunes are being made in the laundry business. An income of $15,000 a year is not uncommon. **Suitable types: 11-22-23-25-30.**

LIBRARIAN

This is one of the professions that offer many intellectual advantages to properly educated and trained men and women, but not so many pecuniary ones. Like the teacher, the librarian is paid less than the exacting requirements of the profession would indicate; but the work is so thoroughly enjoyable that monetary reward becomes of secondary consideration.

A high school diploma is highly essential to even moderate success in this field; but it is generally agreed, among representative librarians of the country, that a college degree is almost vitally important, if one expects to reach the higher places. This is true especially of specialized librarian work, such as the custodianship of a legal or law library, or that of a university or theological school. Public librarians constitute the largest class in the profession, and the intellectual demands in this branch are now greater than ever before.

Since the librarian must read constantly to keep up to date, the profession is highly educational in its scope. Many colleges and universities give special librarian courses, and at Albany, New York, there is an institution which specializes in this branch of training and education alone. Librarians are paid from as low as $900 a year, in smaller cities, to about $10,000 for public librarians in cities like New York, Boston, Philadelphia and Chicago Other branches worthy of consideration are newspaper libraries, now generally recognized as highly valuable adjuncts to all large newspaper offices. Compensation in this branch is somewhat larger than in other library work. **Suitable types: 5-14-15-20-21-24-25-30.**

LUMBER DEALING

To succeed in that phase of the lumber business having to do with big cutting and logging operations, and with the establishment and operation of lumber mills, is absolutely impossible for the man who has not previously had wide experience: hence, the aspirant who desires to enter the business from the outside without beginning at the bottom and working up, should confine his efforts to the retail lumber business.

Even here the newcomer will probably be appalled at the keenness of the competition and the apparently unscrupulous, or "cut-throat" methods employed by competitors to get business. An extraordinarily alert person who understands the fundamental principles of business and is quick witted and decisive enough to act promptly on occasion, stands a fair chance. Otherwise, he would do better to enter the employ of some established lumber firm and, by degrees, gain an insight into the peculiar methods utilized in this branch of endeavor.

The lumber business may show great activity in times of prosperity, and extreme depression at other times. For instance, for years after the World War, and for a long time after building booms had been started in the cities, small town and country lumber yards were absolutely stagnant. Farmers were financially unable to build, and small town residents and business, being dependant upon the farmers' prosperity for their own, were in a similar predicament. The yards located in the cities, therefore enjoyed plenty of patronage, while those in the smaller communities marked time.

Knowledge of shipping facilities, industrial conditions in the timber supply districts and the buying market are the principle essentials to success in retail lumber dealing A yard site, equipped for stacking and seasoning lumber, with an office, will be needed. To establish such a business will cost not less than $10,000 to $15,000, and up. It is one of the most highly competitive businesses in existence. **Suitable types: 7-8-10-11-13-14-20-22-26-19.**

LUMBER BUYING

This is a profession in which competition is not so keen as in the selling of lumber. The supply of expert buyers is limited. The buyer must be able to judge standing forest timber at sight, and to know whether or not it is worth the price demanded. In fact, buyers often fix the prices arbitrarily, paying no attention to the figure names by the owner or agent.

Great lumber mills depend for their profits upon constant operation and a ready market. When the latter is "alive", it is necessary to keep it supplies with all the lumber it will absorb, as there will be periods when sales are virtually impossible. Hence, these mills have corps of buyers always in the timber fields, "scouting" for possible purchases.

In these days of fast working, most mills have their own cutting and logging equipments. Hence, the buyer may purchase whole tracts of standing timber, paying a set sum for it and for the privilege of cutting and logging it. Lumber camps are then set up and gangs of experienced lumbermen transported to the place. In the spring, when the snows begin to melt and the ice goes out of the rivers and creeks, the logs are floated down to their destinations in huge quantities.

The average pay for buyers is $200 to $300 a month in addition to expenses. They usually are graduates of the logging camps. **Suitable types: 11-23.**

MACHINIST

The competent and experienced machinist has two distinctly profitable fields in which to operate: the machine manufacturing, and the machine maintenance. While essentially a trade, it is so a skilled trade that it partakes of the importance of a profession. The machinist may wear overalls and "jumper", but without him an entire shop or factory may have to cease to operations. The "trouble shooter" is quite the most valuable man available at such times. He is like the physician or surgeon: his opinion for the time being is law.

Machinists operate in a very wide field, including all manufacturing and foundry activity, printing, railroading, etc.

Wherever there is machinery there must be a machinist. In the mechanical departments of printing establishments, for instance, where linotype machines are used, the machinist is indispensable. His work consists solely of keeping the linotype machines in operating condition. In factories the machinists are required to look after all machinery used in manufacture. In machine shops, of course, the machinist learns to manufacture parts and to assemble them. The invention and wide manufacture of the automobile has enlarged the field for the machinist.

The aspirant should be of a mechanical turn of mind and like everything pertaining to machinery. He should enjoy diagnosing mechanical trouble, working out mechanical puzzles. The way to get started is by serving an apprenticeship in a technical school or a correspondence school. Technical schools, of course, have facilities for giving the student practical training, while at the same time teaching the theoretical principles.

The aspirant who enters this field, provided he is qualified to become proficient in it, is assured of an excellent income. Experts in large establishments receive up to $350 monthly. As in other lines, however, no "half-baked" machinist ever attains notable
Money-earning place. **Suitable types: 3-10-15 24-25-30**

MANUFACTURER

This is one of the greatest and most profitable of occupations. Henry Ford, the world's richest man, made his wealth in manufacturing. It offers opportunity without limit. The manufacturer should know his business thoroughly. This is of course requisite in all lines, but perhaps more so in manufacturing than in any line of endeavor. Knowledge of raw materials, and their availability at all times; close inspection of and familiarity with both the buying and selling market; ability to select the most skillful labor obtainable; diplomacy to handle threatened labor troubles; knowledge of machinery - these and many other things enter in the problem of profitable manufacturing.

First of all, the manufacturer should make first class goods. But the finest goods in the world will never find their market without the aid of a sales department. Goods must be disposed of at a price above all buying, manufacturing and distributing costs and the only way this can he effectively done is by virtue of clever selling. The factory without a sales force is, in most instances, like a locomotive running uphill on a greased track. Competition is too sharp to admit of the old fashioned way, which was based upon the theory that the world would hunt up the best mousetrap even if it had to make a path through the forest to the door. Nowadays the world waits until the best mousetrap is offered to it by an alert, hard working salesman. If the salesman doesn't materialize, the world will use a mousetrap of less superior maker.

In many lines the factory output is sold through jobbers, or wholesale merchants. The factory's sales force, in such cases will deal almost altogether with these jobbers. Many manufacturing concerns now have big advertising appropriations to create demand for their product. This advertising cost may be shared, to some extent, by the wholesaler and even the retailer.

A manufacturing business may be started in a very small way. The Coca Cola Company had a humble beginning indeed, with one barrel of sugar in stock, and a shed for a factory. The man with faith in himself and the thing he makes, combined with integrity, judgment and a head for business, may succeed in a large way from the smallest of beginnings. **Suitable types: 8-14-15-20-21-23-24-25-27-30-31.**

MANUFACTURER'S AGENT

In all cities of fair size there are many manufacturers' agents, who are the local representatives in the sale and distribution of products. These agents are directly in touch with the headquarters of these products, and communication with a factory concerning the product usually will bring a reply with the manufacturer's agent.

The agent may represent many kinds of products, from as many different manufactories. For instance, the California Fruit company may distribute its products in the city of Denver, and perhaps, in the entire state of Colorado, through an agent located in the capital, who may also be the agent for several other firms scattered all over the United States. The manufacturer's agent, in other words, is the resident representative of the company making the product which he may be handling. He takes the place of a branch office, and is consequently less expensive for the manufacturer to maintain. The manufacturer's agent handles the product on a commission basis, and in return is granted the exclusive privilege of handling it in his territory. He deals with the jobber and wholesale house and frequently directly with the retailer, and thence the consumer.

Most such agents graduate into the business out of retail or wholesale activities, after acquiring the necessary knowledge concerning the products, together with information concerning transportation and shipping facilities, prices, discounts, credits, etc. It is a good business, and for an alert individual can be made to pay large compensation. Many manufacturers' agents clear up to $10,000 and $15,000 annually; many go far beyond this figure. **Suitable types: 11-15-21-24-25-28-29-30-31.**

MARKET GARDENING

Big profits are to be made in this field, by the man who understands the science of market gardening, who is competent in the diagnosis of soil values, and who is capable of producing the highest-grade vegetables for the market. The most successful market gardeners are those who enter the business on a large scale, equipping their gardens with hotbeds, greenhouses, etc.

The "big money" is in the production out of season. In these days the consuming public delights in tomatoes in January, strawberries in December, etc. It will pay three to six times the price asked at seasonable times. Therefore, the gardener able to supply these out-of-season demands, and to produce upon a properly economical basis, may pile up big profits.

A start may be made on a small scale, the venturer enlarging as his business increases. The man who demonstrates real ability in market gardening can usually command capital for expansion purposes, since the market is always available for the gardener who can really produce. The work is hard and exacting, the hours long; but the rewards are good, and the dye-in-the-wool gardener always likes his work.

A three years' course in an agricultural college is a splendid way to start in this field, at a cost, including tuition and living expenses, of approximately $2,500. Correspondence schools also offer agricultural courses, and the Department of Agriculture issues valuable pamphlets and instructions, based upon the results of careful experiments. **Suitable types: 3-13-15-25.**

MILLINERY

This is a business which depends upon seasonal demands for its growth and prosperity more exclusively than any other business catering to the demand for working apparel, and requires a persuasive kind of salesmanship for success. Skilled and rapid workmanship also is required, as well as an artistic bent on the part of the workman and salesman. The combination designer-maker-saleswoman is the most in demand. The best saleswomen are those who can suggest changes which will transform the hat under consideration into exactly what the customer wants, or thinks she wants. **Suitable types: 2-12-24.**

MINING

The mining of coal, metal, and other mineral products is one of this country's basic industries wherein lie splendid opportunities for profitable occupation. The subject is a broad one, covering so many phases as to be impossible to cover in so condensed a space. Schools of Mines, universities and colleges give training on geology and mineralogy that should be the basic education for the young man who loves to handle the products of the earth. The next step is employment with an operating company for experience. The occasional "lucky strike" millionaire of pioneer days is being replaced by the numerous college educated mining man who makes more money and knows how to keep it. **Suitable types: 14-15-25-30-31.**

MOVING AND STORAGE

Wide experience in this business is not so strictly essential as in some other lines. Men who can qualify as fair business men in any other branch of activity may make money in the moving and storage business. Care in the keeping of records, checking and supervision, courtesy in the treatment of patrons, and safe redelivery of articles entrusted to them are the principal requirements for success. In other respects similar methods as employed in many other lines of retail business are sufficient.

Some men start merely by buying a moving van, employing a helper, and advertising in classified newspaper columns for business. A few hundred dollars will suffice. Acquisition of more trucks, and perhaps of the warehouse, may come as the business increases. Launching into the business on a complete scale, with trucks, warehouse, and facilities for storage, will take from $5,000 up, depending on the size and pretentiousness of the business. There is no money to be made in this business except in a managerial or ownership capacity. Employees are paid laborer's wages. Profits accruing to owners, however, may range from $100 up to $1000 per month. **Suitable types: 8-13-19-26.**

NEWS DEALER

This business usually includes the handling of cigars and confectionary. The established news dealer handles everything in print, using judgment as to what publications and papers have the readiest sale, and stocking them up accordingly. Most magazines are consigned to the dealer with a return privilege for unsold copies.

Profits are fair for the man with experience and the right location. Competition is keen almost everywhere. Incomes ranging from $100 a month up to $5000 a year are about an average estimate. Women do well, as do many men who are prevented by physical handicaps from more active work. **Suitable types: 5-6-11-12-14-16-23.**

NURSING

This is one of the most noble of professions and pays fairly well. Nurses must have such an innate sympathy for stricken humanity as to be willing to sacrifice while on duty many of the things the average woman holds dear, such as stylish apparel, social pleasures, periodic travel, etc., for the sake of the unfortunates place in their care. The nurse is the physician's mainstay; without her much of his work would go for naught.

The demand for competent nurses usually exceeds the supply. In times of epidemic the supply is always woefully inadequate. Most babies are now brought into the world in hospitals, which has increased the demand for nurses especially competent to care for such cases. The professional nurse, therefore, is always sure of plenty of employment. Nurses' salaries average from $35.00 to $45.00 weekly, including board. Hospitals maintain schools for student nurses. The student nurse must work the first months without pay, and must expect to perform tasks which the graduate nurse escapes. Graduation takes three years, after which the nurse may be registered and able to command regular professional pay. **Suitable types: 3-7-13-19-20-21-22-26.**

OCULIST

Scientific treatment of diseases of the eye is of vital importance to humanity. The expert oculist fills a great need. His profession differs from that of the optometrist in that the latter merely measures human vision and prescribes lenses of certain strength and degree of concavity or convexity, while the oculist diagnoses ocular disease, treats the eye as a physician may treat any other diseased organ of the body, performs surgical operations on the eyes when required, and also prescribes correct lenses.

Most cities of fair to large size have established clinics, maintained by groups of oculists, and issuing courses in the science of ophthalmology. Many universities now have extension courses in the science, carrying degrees. There are a few schools of ophthalmology in the United States, but they are scattered and available to only a few. The best way for the aspirant to get a start, therefore, is to get in touch with any oculist of standing and make inquiry as to clinical instruction. The applicant should have a college education, or its equivalent. The practice is highly profitable, oculists not being so plentiful as to cause restricting competition. Many oculists have practices paying them $10,000 to $20,000 a year. **Suitable types: 5-8-12-14-15-24-25.**

OPTOMETRY

This is the science of measuring vision and prescribing lenses for correction of the defects. The optometrist's profession and that of the optician are interrelated, the optician being the manufacturer of lenses; therefore the optometrist nearly always has his office in that of an optician, or vice versa. There are large optical manufacturing establishments in many cities, and small town optometrists may take orders for glasses and have them filled at the nearest optical plant, on prescription.

The profits in the business are good, provided enough volume can be secured. Professional optometrists are paid salaries ranging from $45 to $80 weekly. Many schools of optometry now exist in America; inquiry of any optometrist of standing will bring information as to the nearest reliable one. Another way to begin is by the apprenticeship system. **Suitable types: 4-14-15-16-17.**

OSTEOPATHY

Osteopathy is taught in schools established for the purpose. They are located in several states; any osteopath will tell the applicant the location of the nearest reliable one. Osteopathic clinics are also established in most cities of the country, information regarding which is always obtainable from anyone in the profession.

The qualifications for a successful osteopath are cheerfulness, enthusiasm, belief in the efficacy of osteopathy as a curative agent, ability to diagnose symptoms expertly, and dependability. A thorough training in anatomy is necessary, of course. The manipulations taught are peculiar to this science, yet many physicians of other schools learn them also. It will cost not less than $3,000 for the aspiring student to launch himself in the profession, including study and training. Successful osteopaths make incomes from $5,000 up to $25,000 a year. **Suitable types: 13-15-21-24-25-26.**

PATENT ATTORNEY

Patent attorneys are not admitted to patent practice until they have already been admitted to practice before at least one court of record in the United States, and are in good standing with that court. Hence it may be seen that proficiency in both civic and criminal law is required, before one may set up as a patent attorney. In other words, experience in general legal practice must be had before patent practice is permissible, which means that the aspirant must first study law in its fundamental aspects and be admitted to the bar of his state.

Patent attorneys make excellent incomes. One may take the case from the inventor on the usual retainer and fee basis, or he may, if he desires, accept it upon contingent fee basis, taking his pay out of the profits made the manufacture of the invention. Patent attorneys often get in on the ground floor of manufacturing enterprises in this way, and make big incomes. **Suitable types: 15-25-30.**

PHARMACIST

It is a widely quoted expression among those who know, that "drug stores never fail". The profession of pharmacy carries with it the business of drug vending; and this, in turn, carries with it merchandizing activity as varied, almost, as that connected with a modern department store. The pharmacist must, first of all, understand the scientific compounding of medicines and drugs. He must be a graduate and registered pharmacist. He may then obtain a position in a drug store and be permitted to compound prescriptions; or he may, if he has the capital or credit, buy out or establish a drug store of his own.

There are many colleges of pharmacy scattered all over the United States. The logical way to launch one's self upon a pharmaceutical career is to get into touch with one of these schools and arrange for a course in pharmacy. The acquisition of a diploma, and subsequent passing of the state examination, secures for the applicant the essential registration certificate with which he is armed to enter the business. **Suitable types: 5-11-14-15-21-23-24-25-27-28-29-30-31.**

PHOTOGRAPHY

As a profession, photography is now divided into two distinct classifications: "motion" and "still". The latter is subdivided into the "commercial" and "art". The motion picture photographer is called the "camera man". He is in a class by himself, since the motion picture field has little in common with that of "still" photography.

Commercial photographers, or those who specialize in taking pictures of business places and buildings, articles of merchandise for catalog illustrations, show windows, etc., are constantly in demand. Photographers who specialize in taking pictures of large groups of people, such as conventions, may make good incomes. Newspaper photographers with well-developed "news sense" are attached to the staffs of metropolitan dailies, and are sent on assignments to take pictures of train wrecks, automobile wrecks, visiting public men and many other things. Newspaper photographers must be rapid workmen, as speed is highly essential. Art photographers usually are attached to the studios which specialize in portrait work and groups. Good photographers receive salaries ranging from $50 to $80 and $100 per week, depending on the class of activity in which they are engaged. The business is profitable when well established. **Suitable types: 4-8-9-11.**

PHYSICIAN

Strong personalities are essential to success in the treatment of patients; for it is a well known fact that thousands of patients are annually cured more through their faith in the physician than in the efficacy of his medicines. Doctors recognize this, and at their association meetings often discuss the fact. Therefore, it is important that the doctor be a cheerful, optimistic individual, radiating strength and good cheer upon all occasions, and with a clear recognition of the frailties and weaknesses of human character as he finds it.

At least four years in a medical college must be taken by the medical student before he is qualified to enter practice. Constant study, therefore, including the careful perusal of medical journals, attendance upon periodic association meetings and conferences, are equally important.

No one should try to enter the medical profession without financial means enough to pay for a four years' course in medical college. A college education is essential in preparation for the medical course, as well. The physician must be able to purchase a full complement of surgical instruments, since even the doctor who is not a surgeon may be called upon at any time to perform an emergency operation. No young man should expect to launch upon a medical career for an expense of less than $5,000. Those who attain eminence enjoy incomes reaching as high as $50,000 annually. **Suitable types: 9-14-15--20-21-25-27.**

PLUMBING

It is proverbial that the plumber makes a large income, if one may judge from the magnitude of his charges for work performed. The journeyman plumber, however, is not in reality any more highly paid than men in many other trades, but his work is so exacting, and at times so disagreeable, that the remuneration does not loom so large after all.

It is the master plumber who makes the money. This business requires men who know the plumbing trade from the bottom up. No master plumber can hope to succeed if unfamiliar with the trade itself; hence, the way to get a start in the business is to begin as a plumber's apprentice, and gradually work up. After that it is merely a matter of saving or borrowing enough money to make the start. Journeyman plumbers are paid from $50 to $75 a week, with overtime usually offered at additional rates. The master plumber may make from $5,000 a year up. **Suitable types: 7-10-20-21-25-26.**

POULTRY RAISING

As a business, this branch of activity presents a real opportunity for a career for one who likes the work and understands it. Formerly there was no poultry "business". All farmers and many city people kept chickens; there was no information available as to scientific feeding and breeding, as far as the masses were concerned. Chickens just "grew up". But the raising of poultry has taken on such importance in modern times that the government has taken an interest, and the Department of Agriculture periodically issues what approximates a complete correspondence course, so comprehensive are its bulletins regarding the proper way to breed and feed poultry, as well as know how to house them, how to heat the shelters, what degrees of heat will best induce laying, the elimination of vermin, etc.

One of the best methods of gaining information as to the cost of starting this business, equipment necessary, etc., is to write the Department of Agriculture, Washington, D.C., for pamphlets. The inquirer will receive promptly all the information now available, in printed form, the pamphlets illustrated with drawings showing how poultry yards and houses should be constructed, inside and out. **Suitable types: 1-6-7.**

PREACHING

To call the profession of the minister of the gospel a "profitable occupation" might be questioned by many members of the profession. However, there are eminent ministers of Protestant denominations who receive salaries of $10,000 or more; but for each of these there are many hundreds who receive most modest salaries. The preaching profession is in most dire need of recruits. The call for young men to enter the ministry is continuous. While it is undoubtedly true that many men in the pulpit are indifferently equipped for spiritual work, it is equally true that many other men in other lines of activity should by rights be in the pulpit.

There are numerous theological schools and colleges in the United States, and numerous channels of opportunity open to the aspirant. Many churches have a fund out of which divinity students are aided in their college careers, if unable to finance themselves in full. The spirit of self sacrifice must at all times actuate the divinity student, from the beginning to the end of his ministerial career, and thousands are working their way through college in preparation. Without such a spirit the student cannot possibly succeed.

The lot of the minister is better, in a financial sense, than ever before in history. More churches pay comfortable salaries than was the case in former times. Moreover, most ministers actually receive the money due them. **Suitable types: 8-9-14-18-20-23-24.**

PRINTING AND PUBLISHING

Here is a wide and diversified field, with great fortunes being made in it and still to be made, but a business requiring a special brand of enthusiasm, daring and vision for the person who is to succeed in it.

While the publishing business requires the services of expert technicians in a typographical and mechanical sense, there are few big publishers in the world who knew anything about the printing trade when they started. There are some exceptions, which merely prove the rule. United States Senator Arthur Capper, of Topeka, Kan., owns a string of newspapers and magazines with a combined circulation of millions, and Senator Capper got his start at a typesetting case. His experience is exceptional, however. Vanderbilt and other millionaire publishers know practically nothing of the mechanical end of their business.

The publisher of a great metropolitan daily newspaper may clear as high as $1,000,000 a year. The publisher of a country weekly newspaper may consider himself lucky if he is able to pay his help on Saturday night, and extend his credit with the grocer and butcher for another week. Both are publishers, however. The small publisher must have a knowledge of printing in its various branches, especially since the country weekly, or daily pager usually is issued in a "job shop," where orders for handbills are as gladly accepted as anything else.

The small printing establishment may grow to exceedingly large proportions, where weekly papers, magazines and periodicals are printed and where orders are handled for large editions of booklets, folders, pamphlets, "broadsides," etc. The man contemplating entering the publishing business on a modest scale, with the idea of growing larger with experience, opportunity and time, must make his start in the print shop. **Suitable types: 9-14-14-18-20-21-25-27-28-29-30-31.**

PRODUCE DEALER

Also called "commission man". The commission man is the middle man between the farmer or truck gardener, and the retail food distributor, such as the grocer, fruiterer, wholesale vegetable dealer, wholesale grocer, restaurant or hotel owner, etc. The produce dealer necessarily deals in large consignments of produce, which he must dispose of, usually, in not more than twenty-four hours.

Commission men may start in a small way, gradually working up a reputation for integrity and attention to the interests of consignors of produce, and enlarging the business as consignments increase in number and size. A building with railroad switching facilities is essential, refrigeration departments for the care of perishable fruits and vegetables, etc., are highly desirable. Big profits are at times made by produce dealers, while losses must be born occasionally, and expected. The best way to start is to obtain employment in a produce house and gain practical experience in all its branches. Many former employees now have commission businesses of their own. **Suitable types: 6-7-8-10-16-17-19-26-28.**

RAILROADING

The term "railroad" covers men who are employed "on the rails." They include engineers and firemen of locomotives, conductors of freights and passenger trains, brakemen, switchmen, etc. Railroading pays well considering the fact that a thorough academic education is not required. The fireman who receives up to $185 and $225 monthly may become a locomotive engineer, with pay running as high as $350 per month for the rest of his life, up to the time he may be pensioned. The brakeman may become a conductor, his pay then running up to $275 and $300 a month. Freight engineers may get choice passenger runs with trains in their charge. A freight conductor may also advance to command of a passenger train, with corresponding increase in pay and pleasant character of his duties. Train servicemen may be advanced from the ranks into the traffic department, where they may turn out to be material out of which officials are made.

Most railroad presidents in America were once "on the rails", and proud of the fact. Railroad presidents get princely salaries, and travel about in magnificent private cars. Other lesser officials are well paid, from $5,000 up. **Suitable types: Trainmen, 3-10-13-22; Executives, 9-20-21-27-28-29-30-31.**

REAL ESTATE

Probably there is no other business in the United States in which greater fortunes can be made in shorter time, with less capital investment, than the real estate business. It is regarded by many as the highest form of salesmanship, and a field for which there is plenty of room for practical, energetic, honest men and women.

Real estate activities are divided into several classes. The biggest and quickest profits are generally considered to be from the sale of income, or business properties, since large sums of money may be involved in such transactions, with correspondingly large profits. Such income properties as residence apartment houses come next. Some real estate concerns specialize in apartment houses alone, buying and selling, and even building them.

The subdivision is distinctly an American enterprise. From the Atlantic to the Pacific, and from Canada to the Gulf of Mexico, practically every city and town is a prospect for a subdivision. This entails capital for the purchase of a plot of ground, usually running from five to one hundred acres in extent, with streets laid out and graded, sidewalks put in, young trees planted, water, sewer and electric lighting equipment installed, the promoting concern is ready to begin advertising and holding sales of lots. Many companies are well enough financed that they can also build and sell residences on such subdivisions.

While big capital investment is essential to real estate enterprises of this character, salesmen may start in without any money whatever. If they have a car, all the better; if not, the company usually will supply one. What any real estate concern needs is prospective customers, and the salesman who "digs up live prospects" is considered a highly valuable man. Cooperative methods are employed by enterprising firms; that is, the salesman who finds the prospect is aided in the sale by others in the company, and receives a comfortable commission besides.

Real estate men or women usually make a start in the business by opening a small office and gathering together a list of property for sale. Frequently it is possible for enterprise and alert real estate persons to secure exclusive listings, which means that, for a period, no other real estate firm can get credit for selling the property so listed. These listings are accepted with the understanding that the firm is to receive a certain commission on the price obtained. The commission ranges from three to six percent, or the owner may accept a flat price, giving the real estate firm all the money received over that price.

Many real estate concerns represent insurance agencies; some specialize in rentals. Abstracting departments are now maintained by many agencies, where the titles of property under consideration may be ascertained. The rental and leasing agency for big office buildings is a plum for which every enterprising real estate man works, since such connections mean big annual incomes Another important branch of the business is that by which farm and ranch property is dealt in, and this branch requires a knowledge of farm land values, crops reports, etc.

The monetary rewards for the real estate business may be very large indeed. Concerns with net incomes of $100,000 a year are not at all uncommon, especially in the more thickly settled portions of the country. These usually specialize also in loans on approved and unapproved property. The person desiring to enter the real estate business should begin as a salesman. **Suitable types: 11-15-16-20-21-27-28-29-30-31.**

RESTAURANT

Too many persons have the idea that, because people "have to eat", the restaurant business is a sinecure and perfectly safe for anyone who cares to venture into it. This is far from the case. It is in reality one of the most risky businesses in the world, and requires knowledge and experience of a special kind to insure success, even under the most favorable circumstances.

The successful restaurant owner must be skillful at buying foods, including meats and vegetables. In meats, especially, it is possible not only to pay too much, but to lose customers because of the non-edible character of the meat. The buyer of meats for restaurant consumption has a very important mission, and anything but a "snap". He should be able to judge this food expertly.

The cafeteria is replacing many of the old style restaurants and providing quite profitable to qualified proprietors. These seem to offer a special field for women. One of the largest if not the largest chain of cafeterias is the Outra group in Chicago owned by a woman who has made a tremendous success. The cozy tearoom with painted chairs and tables and bizarre ornamentation is another form of restaurant that is becoming decidedly popular in the cities and seems especially the province of women of taste and enterprise. **Suitable types: 1-6-16-17-19-21-26-28.**

SALESMANSHIP

It is said that all human beings, civilized and uncivilized, are in the business of selling something. F. D. Van Amburgh, noted writer and psychologist, says: "Every man has something to sell -- perhaps merchandise, possibly experience, perchance work, mayhap just plain buff... We are all merchants, brokers, bankers, hawkers... From the clerk of the Cabinet, from the user to the usurer, from the buyer to the seller, from the wholesaler to the retailer, all men are concerned in salesmanship." There is a louder call for salesmanship than for any other accomplishment in the field of human endeavor.

The person contemplating a career as a salesman should choose a suitable line. The man who would be successful selling farm implements could not duplicate his success in selling foods. Two entirely different types of persons are required for these two branches. Therefore, the aspirant to the field of salesmanship should carefully ascertain and determine what particular line he is fitted for, by nature, and make his choice accordingly. Basically, however, he must possess these qualities: energy, enthusiasm, knowledge of goods and human nature, sincerity, Self-confidence, optimism, good health, judgment and clarity of thought.

There are numerous ways to get into the selling "game" One is to enter the employ of some manufacturing or wholesale home, to learn the business, for the stated purpose of eventually becoming a salesman of that concern. Practical Experience and familiarity with the stock, prices, etc., are acquired in this way. As a preliminary measure it would be well to take a course in the science and psychology of salesmanship, of which there are many available in the United States, some of them by correspondence. Many large corporations now maintain salesmanship schools, in which they train likely material for "the road." After a salesman has become adept at selling the product or output of one concern, he may find himself equipped to sell many kindred things, and able to hold positions in other selling lines.

Salesmen on the road seldom draw less than $150 monthly, together with all expenses, including railroad or automobile transportation, hotels, etc. As they progress in selling ability and acquaintance with the "trade" they may advance in proportion in compensation, until they reach as high as $1,000 a month. Super-salesmen, representing great corporations, receive as high as $100,000 annually. **Suitable types: Foods, 1-6-7-8-16-17-18-36-28-29-31; Art and sporting goods, 2-11-12-16-17-18-23-24-28-29-31; Fabrics, clothes, furniture, hardware, machinery, 11-14-22-23-24-30; Securities: 11-14-16-22-23-29.**

SHORTHAND REPORTING

To the man or woman with a capacity for close application, hard work, extreme accuracy and a "working" knowledge of law and legal phraseology, short hand reporting offers a highly lucrative field for a career. Reporters of court procedure, depositions of testimony, etc., often make very large fees and are certain of steady employment as long as they want it. Not only are such reporters used in reporting legal proceedings of every kind, but they are in keen demand for the reporting of congressional and senatorial hearings, special investigations, recording and transcribing of criminal confessions and many other things of similar character. Accuracy is highly essential.

A close study of short hand by any one of the standard systems must be undertaken, to start. Many aspirants take courses in business colleges, schools, colleges and universities. Others study by the correspondence method, and still others merely buy short hand textbooks and proceed to wrest the necessary knowledge out for themselves. Efficiency in shorthand reporting is largely a matter of experience and practice. In addition to accuracy, speed is imperative. Aspirants usually get this experience by attending court hearings and taking down testimony for practice. Much valuable experience may be gained through stenographic connection with law firms. **Suitable types: 5-9-14-15-24-30.**

STEAM FITTING

The growth of apartment houses, family hotels and steam-heated places generally has made the trade of the steamfitter indispensable. The steamfitter is a skilled laborer, in a sense; but the man who has foresight, business ability and thrift can advance from the ranks of the trade worker into the realm of business, taking steamfitter contracts and selling steam fitters' supplies, at good profit. A contracting steamfitter is able to add to his profits if he is also in the business of selling supplies, since he will then be able to bid on the basis of wholesale costs of these supplies.

The steam fitter's profession is now taught in technical and correspondence schools, at nominal cost. The aspirant may attain work in a shop as an apprentice, and supplement his practical experience with technical study. The worker at the trade may be paid from eight to ten dollars a day; if he enters business for himself he may make twice this sum. **Suitable types: 7-19-20-21-25-26.**

STOREKEEPING

Store keeping is one of the most extensive of businesses. The merchant may start with small capital, or with large, depending on the ambitious character of the undertaking. The boy who sells newspapers on the street is a merchant. The late John Wanamaker, with millions of dollars invested in his great stores of Philadelphia and New York City, was a merchant. In between these two extremes are hundreds of thousands of enterprises, ranging from an investment of a few dollars to millions.

The aspirant should first select a line of nature with which he is by nature congenial. If he has been able to master a theoretical course in business, such as may be purchased from any business college, school or university, so much the better. Organization and other business fundamentals must be learned, either by study or by practical experience. The merchant should study constantly, even after he is launched in business, if he is to reach the higher places in this line of activity.

The cost of getting into either the wholesale or retail business varies with the line, location, extent of the enterprise, and many other things. The profits cannot be measured in advance. Suffice it to say that some of the richest men in the United States are in these lines. **Suitable types: Foods, 1-6-7-17-19-21-26-27-28; Art and Sporting goods, 10-11-12-18-23-24-30; Jewelry, 14; Fabrics and clothes, 6-7-8-9-11-20-25-27; Furniture and hardware, 14-15-23-24-25-30.**

SURGEON

This is the day of operations. Modern medicine has made possible the saving of many lives through surgery. Where in former times people have died with appendicitis, for example, under the impression that they were suffering from "inflammation of the bowels" now go under the surgeon's knife for the expert removal of the little organ known as the appendix, and recover to live long and presumably happy lives thereafter.

Preparation for a career in surgery is, to a large extent, parallel to that for the medical profession. The surgeon usually is the "doctor, plus." It is unnecessary to stress the fact that the surgeon must possess all the psychological equipment of the doctor, and in addition steady nerves. Very few men can ever become successful surgeons. As with the doctor, the surgeon must go through a long period of study and training, and must he a college graduate, or have an education the equivalent to it, before he can qualify for entrance into a school of medicine and surgery. Not less than $5,000 should be available for this preparatory period. **Suitable types: 14-23-30.**

TEACHING

With the public impulse for education sowing rapidly in the United States, the demand for competent teachers and educators in the great public school systems, normal schools, colleges and universities is now greater than ever before in history, with public appreciation reflected in ever increasing salaries. Nearly 700,000 teachers, including principals, are now employed in the nation's public school system, the total annual operating expense of which was $864,396,526 in 1920, and close to $900,000,000 in 1923. A very large part of this expenditure is of course represented in teachers' salaries.

A high school education is sufficient to start the young man or woman in teaching in the intermediate grades, although a college education is better. Teachers' examinations are held periodically in central districts all over the United States; the minimum age limits for those who may be awarded certificates range from seventeen years upward. Applications for schools or positions cannot be entertained, in most places, unless the applicant be armed with a certificate. The teacher-student may take any examination, of whatever grade, for which he or she may be considered qualified; many start with the lowest and gradually work up the scale. Postgraduate courses may he taken to equip the teacher for the higher educational positions, where the salaries are commensurate with the educational and pedagogical requirements.

Salaries range from $600 a year in some states and districts; up to $25,000 annually for the educational heads of school districts in the greater cities. The average for city schoolteachers is about $1200 to $2400 a year, paid monthly, with no exceptions for vacation periods. Men or women with A. M. degrees are paid $3,000 a year or better. In the colleges salaries run higher.

The teaching profession is one that should attract the ambitious man or woman with enough education to make the start, since it is undoubtedly offering greater attractions from every standpoint, as time goes on. Suitable types: 5-14-15-20-21-23-24-25-30-31; Music, 6-15-17-18.

TRADES

The following list enumerates fifty various trades that require skill and training with suitable types for each.

Baker	1-6-7-8
Billing Clerk	4-11
Blacksmith	3-4-13
Boilermaker	3-4-13
Bookbinder	3-4-13
Bookkeeper	4-5-11-14
Brakeman	3-10-11
Bricklayer	3-4-13
Carpenter	3-4-13
Clerk, Groceries	1-2-3-6-7
Clerk, Drugs	2-4-11
Clerk, Dry Goods	4-11
Clerk, Clothing	2-11
Clerk, Hardware	3-4-10-11-13
Clerk, Office	4-11
Compositor	3-4
Conductor	4-10-11
Cook	1-7
Credit man	4-14
Draftsman	4-5-10-11-14-15
Engraver	3-4
Estimator	4-5-11
Fireman	4-13

Foundry man	3-4-13
Jewelry	4
Lineman	10-11
Linotype Operator	3-4-10-11-13
Locomotive Engineer	3-4-10-11-13
Machine Operator	3-10-13
Mechanic	3-10-13
Miner	3-4-13
Motorman	3-4-10-11-13
Office Manager	4-9-11-14-15
Paper Hanger	3-4-10-11-13
Painter	3-4-10-11-13
Photo Engraver	3-4-10-11-13-15
Plasterer	3-4-13
Policeman	10-22
Pressman	3-4-10-11-13
Seaman	10-22
Steel Worker	10-22
Shipping Clerk	3-4-13
Stationary Engineer	3-4-13
Stenographer	5-10-11-12-14-15
Stone Mason	3-4-10-13-22
Timekeeper	4-11
Tinner	3-4-13
Watchmaker	4

TRAFFIC MANAGEMENT

The demand for men specializing in this branch of railroad work has of late years been more or less keen, depending upon national economic conditions. Familiarity with traffic conditions that prevail in the United States and Canada is required. The traffic manager must know the usual methods of handling and tracing freight, and dealing with claims. The origin and principals of freight classifications, also class rates within and between classification territories, must be learned.

Other things to be known by the traffic man are interpretations of interstate commerce laws, rules and regulations, correct readings and applications of tariffs, etc. In other words, the expert traffic man is who is thoroughly familiar with such intricate things as govern the transportation of freight from one end of the North American Continent to the other, and ocean transportations as well.

A high school education is usually sufficient for the applicant. Many universities give special traffic courses, also correspondence schools. Such courses may be purchased for about $150 to $175 each. Payment for the traffic expert may run as high as $7,500 a year, relatively good salaries being paid the new graduate who obtains his first position. The young man with the requisite knowledge may be reasonably certain of being paid at least $25 to $30 a week, at the start, and promotion is usually steady and sure. **Suitable types: 5-14-15-25.**

UNDERTAKING

The successful undertaker, who may also be called a "mortician" or "funeral director," is the one who combines skill in embalming and other expert care of human bodies, with tact of a high degree, sympathy, kindliness and courtesy. In many respects this is a most highly specialized business. Many who qualify as experts in the care of bodies are unqualified to direct funerals because they lack the personalities essential to success.

The undertaker who hopes to succeed must he able to command sufficient capital to carry him over slow-pay periods represented by impecunious clients. In many ways it is a very hazardous business. There is neither time nor opportunity for the undertaker to investigate the financial standing of the applicant, and the money losses on poor risks are large. For this reason the fees charged seem out of all proportion to the service rendered.

The undertaker cannot decline to serve an applicant, even though he may be morally certain that he will never be paid. Such an attitude would be a violation of the professional code of ethics. Hence the risk - and the high prices charged. Those who pay in full must bear the burden represented by those who do not.

The undertaker must first serve an apprenticeship, before he is qualified to go into business for himself. He must understand the art of embalming and care of bodies. Many undertakers have become wealthy. Expert embalmers and other assistants are paid from $35 a week up to $3,000 a year. Owners of establishments make as high as $100,000 a year. The best way to start is an employee in an established business, and work up. **Suitable types: 18.**

WRITING

Authorship covers several distinct fields, all of which are profitable to those who develop proficiency. These are: journalism or work on the editorial and reportorial staffs of newspapers: press agent, doing publicity work for stage people, public men or business enterprises; magazine editorial work, reading and buying manuscripts; magazine writing, fiction or descriptive and novel writing, play writing, song writing, scenario writing and the preparation of text books and books on other subjects. Most writers work on salaries. The rest sell their shorter works to magazines and have their books published on a royalty basis. Successful authorship requires a good education and years of hard, drudging work. **Suitable types: 5-14-15-23-25-30.**

We Have Book Recommendations for You

The Strangest Secret by Earl Nightingale (Audio CD)

Acres of Diamonds [MP3 AUDIO] [UNABRIDGED] (Audio CD)
by Russell H. Conwell

Automatic Wealth: The Secrets of the Millionaire Mind -
Including: Acres of Diamonds, As a Man Thinketh, I Dare you!,
The Science of Getting Rich, The Way to Wealth, and Think and
Grow Rich [UNABRIDGED]
by Napoleon Hill, et al (CD-ROM)

Think and Grow Rich [MP3 AUDIO] [UNABRIDGED]
by Napoleon Hill, Jason McCoy (Narrator)   (Audio CD)

As a Man Thinketh [UNABRIDGED]
by James Allen, Jason McCoy (Narrator) (Audio CD)

Your Invisible Power: How to Attain Your Desires by Letting
Your Subconscious Mind Work for You [MP3 AUDIO]
[UNABRIDGED]

Thought Vibration or the Law of Attraction in the Thought
World [MP3 AUDIO] [UNABRIDGED]
by William Walker Atkinson, Jason McCoy (Narrator)
(Audio CD)

The Law of Success Volume I: The Principles of Self-Mastery by
Napoleon Hill (Audio CD)

The Law of Success, Volume I: The Principles of Self-Mastery
(Law of Success, Vol. 1) (The Law of Success) by Napoleon Hill
(Paperback)

Thought Vibration or the Law of Attraction in the Thought
World & Your Invisible Power (Paperback)

The Richest Man in Babylon: Now Revised and Updated
☐   for the 21st Century (Paperback) ☐☐by George S. Clason

Automatic Wealth, The Secrets of the Millionaire Mind - Including: As a Man Thinketh, The Science of Getting Rich, The Way to Wealth and Think and Grow Rich (Paperback)

The Bestsellers in this Book give sound advice about money and how to obtain it. Just reach for the stars, stay focused on your dreams, and watch them come true. There is nothing we can imagine that we can't do. So what are we waiting for? Let's begin the journey of self-fulfillment.

4 Bestsellers in 1 Book:

As a Man Thinketh by James Allen

The Science of Getting Rich by Wallace D. Wattles

The Way to Wealth by Benjamin Franklin

Think and Grow Rich by Napoleon Hill

www.bnpublishing.com

NOTES

BN Publishing

Improving People's Life

www.bnpublishing.com

NOTES

NOTES

BN Publishing

Improving People's Life

www.bnpublishing.com

NOTES

BN Publishing

Improving People's Life

www.bnpublishing.com

NOTES

BN Publishing

Improving People's Life

www.bnpublishing.com

NOTES

BN Publishing

Improving People's Life

www.bnpublishing.com